Serial Killers Unsolved

10 Terrifying Serial Killers
Who Got Away with Murder

Robert Keller

**Please Leave Your Review of This Book At
http://bit.ly/kellerbooks**

ISBN-13: 978-1535212342
ISBN-10: 1535212349

Table of Contents

Zodiac

It started on a cold Friday evening in December 1968. David Arthur Faraday, 17, and Betty Lou Jensen, 16, had told their parents that they were going to attend a Christmas concert. Instead, they drove to a stretch of Lake Herman Road, near Vallejo, California, a well-known make-out spot. They'd been parked there less than an hour, when someone pulled in behind them, driving a light-colored Chevrolet. The driver exited his vehicle and walked towards Faraday's Rambler. Then, without warning, he produced a .22 pistol and began firing.

The killer started from behind the vehicle, shooting out the rear window, then the left rear tire, then coming around to the front left as the teenagers scrambled out of the passenger side door.

Jensen managed to get out of the vehicle and started running towards the road, but she'd made less than 30 feet when she was shot in the back. The killer then shot her five more times, apparently as she lay on the ground. Faraday didn't even make it that far. He was killed by a single bullet, fired at close range into his head. His body was found beside the right rear wheel.

The entire episode was over in seconds and the killer fled the scene immediately. Just minutes later, another driver arrived on the scene and found the bodies of the two teenagers. She rushed to

call the police, but by then it was too late. Jensen and Faraday were
already dead.

A massive investigation was launched, led by Solano County Det.
Sgt. Les Lundblad, and supported by half a dozen local law
enforcement agencies. It turned up nothing. Neither did a reward
fund, set up by students at the victims' high schools, help in finding
the killer. There were no witnesses, no apparent motive, no
suspects.

Six months after the Faraday / Jensen murders, Darlene Elizabeth
Ferrin, 22, and Michael Renault Mageau, 19, were parked at the
Blue Rock Springs Golf Course in Benicia. The golf course was four
miles from where the previous murders had occurred. At around
midnight, a car, a brown Ford Mustang or Chevy Corvair pulled up
behind the couple's vehicle. The driver turned off his headlights
and sat there in the dark, with the car engine idling. A moment
later the car pulled away and drove back towards Vallejo at high
speed.

But five minutes later, the car was back, this time parking behind
Ferrin's vehicle blocking the exit. A man got out of the car and
approached. He was carrying a bright flashlight, which blinded
Mageau and Ferrin and prevented them from seeing his face.
Believing him to be a police officer, Mageau reached for his I.D.
He'd barely moved when the man raised a gun and fired five
rounds in quick succession. The first shots hit Mageau in the face
and body, the bullets fired at such close range that they tore
through his flesh and entered Ferrin.

Mageau managed to get into the back seat as another bullet hit him in the left knee and the attacker then turned the gun on Ferrin hitting her once in each arm and in the back. The killer then walked back to his vehicle but returned when he heard Mageau cry out in pain. He fired two more shots at each victim, then turned and walked casually away.

A moment after he fled the scene three teenagers pulled into the lot and found the grievously wounded couple. Several police cars and an ambulance were soon on the scene. Mageau and Ferrin were evacuated to Kaiser Foundation Hospital, where Mageau was immediately rushed into surgery. Darlene Ferrin was not as lucky. She was pronounced Dead on Arrival.

Michael Mageau was later able to provide a description of the killer. He said the man was about 5-foot-8 and heavyset, with a large face.

At 12:40 that same night, a call was placed via the operator to the Vallejo Police Department. The caller's voice was mature and without a discernible accent, and he spoke evenly, as though reading from a script.

"I want to report a double murder," he said. "If you go one mile east on Columbus Parkway to the public park, you will find kids in a brown car. They were shot with a 9 mm Luger. I also killed those kids last year. Good bye."

The call was traced and found to have come from a pay phone on the corner of Tuolumne Street and Springs Road, just a few blocks away from the Vallejo Sheriff's Office.

A few weeks after the latest murders, on Friday, August 1, 1969, the San Francisco Examiner, San Francisco Chronicle and Vallejo Times-Herald each received an almost identical letter, purportedly from the person responsible for the attacks. Also included was a mysterious cipher, one-third of the puzzle sent to each newspaper. The author demanded that the letters be published on the front page of each newspaper by that Friday afternoon. If his demand was not met, he said, he'd go on a killing spree and kill a dozen random people over the weekend. The letters were signed with a crossed-circle symbol.

The authorities weren't taking any chances. The letters along with the ciphers were published as demanded. However, the police decided to try and draw the killer out and perhaps lure him into making a mistake. In order to do this, investigators stated publicly that they believed the letters to be a hoax. It worked. On August 4, 1969, another letter arrived at the San Francisco Examiner.

The letter began with the chilling salutation that would become the killer's calling card:

"This is the Zodiac speaking…"

It was the first time the killer used the name Zodiac. He went on to provide details about the crimes that had not been released publicly, thereby establishing his authenticity. He also stated that there was a clue to his identity in the ciphers he'd sent with the previous letters.

Frantic efforts were currently underway to decipher those puzzles, but when the answer came it was not a police code-cracker who solved it, but a high school teacher and his wife. They presented their solution on August 8, 1969, having been able to decode all but the last 18 letters.

The message read:

I LIKE KILLING PEOPLE BECAUSE IT IS SO MUCH FUN IT IS MORE FUN THAN KILLING WILD GAME IN THE FORREST BECAUSE MAN IS THE MOST DANGEROUE ANAMAL OF ALL TO KILL SOMETHING GIVES ME THE MOST THRILLING EXPERENCE IT IS EVEN BETTER THAN GETTING YOUR ROCKS OFF WITH A GIRL THE BEST PART OF IT IS THAE WHEN I DIE I WILL BE REBORN IN PARADICE AND THEI HAVE KILLED WILL BECOME MY SLAVES I WILL NOT GIVE YOU MY NAME BECAUSE YOU WILL TRY TO SLOI DOWN OR ATOP MY COLLECTIOG OF SLAVES FOR MY AFTERLIFE EBEORIETEMETHHPITI.

The cipher did not, as promised contain any clues to the killer's identity, although amateur sleuths and code-crackers have since claimed that the letters can be rearranged to spell "Robert Emmet the Hippie."

Zodiac's next attack occurred on Saturday, September 27, 1969, at Lake Berryessa in Napa County, some 60 miles northeast of San Francisco. College students, Cecelia Ann Shepard and Bryan Calvin

Hartnell, were picnicking at Twin Oak Ridge, a peninsula on the western shore of the lake. It was late afternoon when they spotted a man walking towards them, later described as 5-foot-8 to 6-foot tall, dark-haired and heavyset, wearing glasses and dressed in dark clothing.

As the man got closer, he suddenly ducked behind the cover of some trees. When he emerged again, he was just 20 feet away and had slipped on a strange four-cornered hood, black in color, with a bib that fell almost to his waistline. Embroidered on the bib was a crossed-circle design. He had a pistol in his hand and a long knife hung from his belt.

The man told the terrified couple that he was an escaped convict from Montana   and that he wanted money and their car to drive to Mexico. Hartnell immediately handed over his keys and all the change from his pockets. The man pocketed the change and dropped the keys on the picnic basket. Hartnell then engaged the man in conversation, in an effort to calm him down, and they spoke for a few minutes. Then the man removed some clothesline from his belt and ordered Shepard to tie Hartnell up. Hartnell tried to reason with him, but the man became angry and shouted: "Get down! Right now!"

Shepard then tied Hartnell up as the man had instructed, after which she herself was bound. Hartnell would later say that the man appeared nervous, his hands shaking. "I'm going to have to stab you people," he said.

"I couldn't stand to see her stabbed," Hartnell responded. "Stab me first."

"I'll do just that," the killer replied.

Hartnell was stabbed six times, Shepard ten, the weapon used, a double-edged blade approximately 12-inches long. Leaving them for dead, the killer then walked to Hartnell's car, parked nearby. Using a black magic marker, he made the following inscription:

Vallejo

12-20-68

7-4-69

Sept 27-69-6:30

by knife

He also drew the crossed-circle emblem that would feature on his subsequent letters.

As he had after the previous attack, the killer drove to a pay phone and placed a call via the operator to the police. The Napa Police Department switchboard logged the call at 7:40 pm, a little over an hour after the attack. "I want to report a murder - no, a double murder," the killer said. "They are two miles north of Park Headquarters. They were in a white Volkswagen Kharmann Ghia."

"Where are you calling from?" the switchboard operator asked.

"I'm the one that did it," the caller said, before dropping the receiver and walking away.

Bryan Hartnell would recover from his wounds, but Cecelia Ann Shepard would succumb to hers two days later. Zodiac would never refer to this attack again.

On the night of Saturday, October 11, 1969, San Francisco cab driver Paul Stine picked up a fare at the corner of Mason and Geary Streets in Union Square. The passenger asked to go to the Presidio, at the northern tip of the San Francisco peninsula. However, the cab traveled just one block before pulling to the curb at the corner of Washington and Cherry Streets. Here, the passenger shot Stine point blank in the right side of the head. He then got into the front seat, removed the dead man's wallet and keys, and cut a large piece from the back of his shirt which he soaked in blood, taking it with him as he walked slowly north on Cherry Street.

Three teenage siblings standing at a second-floor window of 3899 Washington, saw the killer cut Stine's shirt, then exit the cab and wipe down the door handles and parts of the cab's interior. The boys suspected something amiss and called the police, who logged the call at 9:58 pm and immediately dispatched a cruiser. However, the description of the killer was incorrectly broadcast as a black male. As a result, when patrolmen Donald Foukes and Eric Zelms noticed a heavyset, white man walking casually east on Jackson Street, they made no effort to apprehend him.

Two days after the murder of Paul Stine, the Chronicle received a letter from Zodiac claiming responsibility for the murder. A swatch of Stine's bloody shirt was enclosed. "This is the Zodiac speaking," the letter began. "I am the murderer of the taxi driver over by Washington St + Maple St last night…"

He went on to criticize the police, saying they would have caught him if they'd searched the area properly, instead of " holding road races with their motorcycles seeing who could make the most noise." He then issued a chilling threat. His next victims, he said, would be a busload of school children.

The Zodiac case had by now begun to garner massive media coverage, and tips as to the killer's identity started coming in from as far afield as Houston, Atlanta, and St. Louis. At the same time, homicide detectives along the West Coast began to look at their unsolved cases for possible links to the killer. One of those was the brutal killing of Cheri Jo Bates in Riverside, California.

Bates had been slashed and stabbed to death outside the Riverside City College Library on the night of Sunday, October 30, 1966. The killer had apparently disabled her car by pulling out the distributor coil and condenser. Then he waited for her to return, whereupon he stepped forward like a knight in shining armor and offered to help. After pretending to tinker with the engine he declared that he couldn't start the vehicle and offered a ride, which Bates accepted. He then somehow lured her to a darkened area between two houses, which was where her body was found next morning. She'd been slashed across the back, chest and throat, the latter wounds running so deep that they almost decapitated her. She had also been choked, beaten, and slashed across the face.

There were plenty of clues left at the scene. The police found a man's Timex watch close by and a heel-print from a man's shoe. There was hair, blood, and skin tissue found under the victim's fingernails and unidentified palm and fingerprints found in and on her car. Then there were two separate witnesses who reported hearing an "awful scream" at around 10:30. This tied in with the time of death estimated by the coroner and was regarded as a significant clue by investigators. The library closed at 9:00, and if the murder occurred at 10:30 that meant Cheri Jo Bates had spent an hour and a half sitting in the car with her killer. That suggested that he was known to her and, given the brutal ferocity of the attack, the police believed that the killer might be a spurned ex-boyfriend. They were confident of an early arrest.

But a month passed with no arrest and very little progress in the case. Then, on November 29, 1966, two copies of the same anonymous letter were delivered to the Riverside Police and the Riverside Enterprise newspaper. Entitled "The Confession," it contained a graphic description of the Bates murder, including some details that had not been made public. In other key aspects, though, the author was wrong. Nonetheless, the letter got investigators no closer to solving the murder.

Six months after the death of Cheri Bates, the police, Riverside Press, and the victim's father were each sent near identical copies of another letter. This one was written in pencil on lined notepaper and contained a unique "signature," a letter Z joined with a numeral 3. The letters read as follows:

BATES HAD

TO DIE

THERE WILL

BE MORE

A couple of weeks later, a janitor at the Riverside City College Library discovered a poem written on the underside of a folding school desk. The content seemed to refer to the Bates murder but as with the other clues, this one led nowhere.

The Bates murder has never been solved and continues to divide opinion. Riverside PD maintains that a local man was the key suspect, not the Zodiac. Other investigators, both professional and lay, insist that Cheri Jo Bates was Zodiac's first victim.

On October 22, 1969, a caller identifying himself as the Zodiac called the Oakland Police Department and demanded time on the Jim Dunbar TV talk show with either F. Lee Bailey or Melvin Belli, both famous defense lawyers. Belli agreed to appear and, during the show someone, claiming to be Zodiac, did call. However, it was later determined that the call was a hoax.

The next two Zodiac letters arrived at the Chronicle on November 8 and November 9. The first contained a 340-character cipher. The second was a seven-page missive, which included another piece of Stine's shirt. In this letter, Zodiac claimed that police officers had stopped him on the night of the Stine murder and had questioned him for three minutes before letting him go. The SFPD vehemently denied this. The letter also contained a schematic for a "death machine," which was to be used to blow up buses.

Zodiac's next communication was a Christmas card sent to Melvin Belli's home on December 20, 1969. In the card the Zodiac begged Belli for help, with the words:

"Please help me I can not remain in control for much longer."

Most of the investigators working the case saw this for what it was, another attempt by Zodiac to garner media attention. However, Belli took the message seriously and made full use of the free publicity it afforded him and his legal practice with a number of very public attempts to reach out to the Zodiac. The Zodiac never contacted him again. In fact, nothing more was heard from the killer for three months.

On the evening of Sunday, March 22, 1970, 23-year-old Kathleen Johns was driving to meet her mother. Her ten-month-old daughter, Jennifer, was also in the car. Along a stretch of Highway 132 near Modesto, a man in a light-colored car started honking his horn and blinking his lights at her. Driving alongside he indicated that there was a problem with one of her wheels. Johns pulled over to the side of the highway and the man pulled up beside her. He said that her wheel was wobbling and offered to fix it for her. He then fetched a lug wrench and got to work. In fact, there was nothing wrong with the wheel at all, and rather than tightening the lugs, the man loosened them. When Johns tried to drive off, the wheel came off. The man was not far ahead and now backed up and offered a ride to the nearest gas station. Johns gratefully accepted.

However, she was soon to regret her decision. The man continued west along 132, but it soon became clear that he had no intention of taking her to a gas station as he passed several without stopping. Terrified for her safety, and that of her daughter, Johns endured an hour and a half of aimless driving through the city of Tracy and its environs. She tried to engage the man in conversation but he was mostly silent. "Do you always go around helping people?" she asked at one point. "By the time I get through with them, they won't need my help," the man responded. She began to realize that if she didn't try to escape both she and Jennifer were going to be killed. Finally, she saw her chance. As the man brought the car to a halt at a stop sign, she grabbed Jennifer and jumped from the car. She ran across a field and up an embankment, taking cover in the shadows. Depending on which version of Johns' subsequent story you believe, the man either waited in his car for a few minutes or came looking for her with a flashlight. Either way, he eventually gave up and drove off.

Johns was picked up by a passing motorist, who took her to the police station in Patterson. As she entered she saw a Wanted poster with a composite sketch of the Zodiac and insisted that he was the man who had abducted her. Meanwhile, a call went out to locate her car. A Stanislaus County Sheriff's Deputy found it where it had been left, burned out and still smoldering - the abductor had returned to torch the vehicle.

The abduction attempt marked the last time anyone ever reported seeing the Zodiac. However, his letter-writing campaign would continue for some time. The next missive arrived at the San Francisco Chronicle on April 20, 1970. It included a 13-character cipher, a diagram of a bomb he planned to use to blow up a school bus, and a statement that he was not involved in the February 18 bombing of a San Francisco police station. The letter ended with a note "Zodiac=10, SFPD=0." (Zodiac was indicated not by the word, but by the now familiar crossed circle.) The police believed that 10 indicated the number of people the Zodiac was claiming to have killed.

Just over a week later, on April 28, 1970, a card arrived at the Chronicle with the words, "I hope you enjoy yourselves when I have my BLAST." The writer threatened to use his bus bomb if the Chronicle failed to publish the April 20 letter, detailing his plans to blow up a school bus. He also requested that people start wearing Zodiac buttons.

Another letter to the Chronicle, received on June 26, contained a 32-letter cipher. The author said he was upset that no one was wearing Zodiac buttons. He also took credit for another shooting, which investigators believed to be the murder of police Sergeant Richard Radetich, a week earlier. However, eyewitnesses to that murder reported that the shooter had been a black man.

Also included was a map of the Bay area, supposedly giving clues to a bomb that he'd buried, which was due to detonate in the fall.

This letter was signed "Zodiac=12. SFPD=0."

The next letter arrived at the Chronicle a month later. In it, the Zodiac claimed responsibility for abducting Kathleen Jones four months earlier.

Zodiac was on a roll now - the next letter arrived just a couple of days later on July 26, 1970. In it, he included a twisted version of the song "I've Got a Little List" from the Gilbert & Sullivan musical, "The Mikado." The stylized lyrics described how he intended torturing his slaves. He concluded with an update on the "score," Zodiac=13, SFPD=0.

Three months passed before the next Zodiac communiqué arrived on October 5, 1970. It consisted of a card with letters cut from magazines and newspapers. Thirteen holes were punched through the card, thought to represent the number of victims. This card was originally thought to be a hoax but would later gain credence among Zodiac researchers.

Two days later a card, ostensibly from the Zodiac, was sent to Paul Avery, the Chronicle's main reporter on the case. It included a threat to Avery's life. Days later Avery received a letter urging him to investigate the murder of Cheri Jo Bates as part of the Zodiac series.

In March 1971, Zodiac spread his wings, addressing a letter to the Los Angeles Times. He claimed he was writing to the Times because "They don't bury me on the back pages."

In the letter, the Zodiac gave the police credit for connecting him to the Bates murder, but insisted that they were only finding the "easy ones" and that there were "plenty more out there." The letter concluded with the score, SFPD=0 Zodiac=17.

He returned to familiar territory on March 22, 1971, sending a postcard to

Paul Avery in which he claimed responsibility in the disappearance of a nurse, Donna Lass, who'd gone missing from the Sahara Hotel and Casino. Some investigators believed that the postcard was a forgery, perhaps an attempt by the real killer to make the authorities believe Lass was a Zodiac victim. However, certain idiosyncrasies point to its authenticity. The use of punch holes was a Zodiac trait, as was the misspelling of Paul Avery's name as "Averly."

This postcard was the last communication received from the Zodiac for three years. By the time the next letter arrived on January 29, 1974, he'd dropped his familiar salutation, "This is the Zodiac speaking." The cross-circle symbol signature was also gone.

In this letter, he describing the movie, The Exorcist, as "the best saterical comidy that I have ever seen." He also included part of a verse from "The Mikado," and a hieroglyph-type drawing. He threatened to "do something nasty" if the letter wasn't published and concluded with the score, "Me-37 SFPD-0."

On May 8, 1974, the Chronicle received a letter from a "concerned citizen" complaining about the violence in the movie "Badlands." Although the Zodiac did not identify himself as the author, many Zodiac experts believe the tone of the letter and the handwriting was unmistakably that of the Zodiac.

Another disputed letter arrived on July 8, 1974. It complained about Chronicle columnist, Marco Spinelli, and was signed, "the

Red Phantom (red with rage)." Police Detective David Toschi sent the letter to the FBI Lab for analysis. They responded that the letter probably came from whoever had written the Zodiac letters. There would be no further communication from the Zodiac for four years.

On April 24, 1978, a letter arrived at the Chronicle purporting to be from the Zodiac. The letter was given to reporter Duffy Jennings, who forwarded it to Detective Toschi, the only SFPD Officer still working the Zodiac case.

Toschi sent the letter to John Shimoda of the U.S. Postal Service crime laboratory, and Shimoda came back verifying it as genuine. However, four other experts declared the letter a hoax and even suggested that Toschi had written it himself.

Genuine or not, the Toschi letter was the last communication from the Zodiac. Why, exactly, he chose to stop taunting the police is as much of a mystery as his identity.

But who was the Zodiac? There is no shortage of suspects, more than 2, 500 interviewed over the course of the investigation. Yet one name dominates the suspect lists, the favorite of many investigators, as well as Robert Graysmith, author of the seminal book on the case, "ZODIAC."

Arthur Leigh Allen was a Vallejo resident and convicted pedophile. He first came to the attention of the Vallejo Police Department in early October 1969 and was later named by two separate people (a former friend, and a former cellmate) as the Zodiac. Yet the case against Allen disintegrates under closer scrutiny. In fact, much of the information linking Allen to the case has been proven to be either untrue or highly circumstantial. When you consider that Allen was too tall to match eyewitness descriptions; that he had solid alibis for many of the crimes; that he passed a grueling 10-hour polygraph; and that DNA evidence lifted from the Zodiac letters was categorically proven not to be from him, it is difficult to sustain the belief that he was the Zodiac.

Allen died in 1992, but the case remains unsolved and is likely to keep true crime aficionados intrigued for decades to come.

The Mad Butcher of Kingsbury Run

Kingsbury Run is a ravine that cuts across the east side of Cleveland. Nearly sixty feet deep in places, it is a barren wasteland that empties eventually into the cold waters of the Cuyahoga River. Back in the 1930's this area was home to a large community of nomadic, destitute folk, dumped there by the Great Depression. Squat cardboard and tin shacks leaned to among the patches of scrub grass, weeds, garbage and abandoned, rusting old cars, while closer to the river, an array of blackened factory buildings belched sulfurous, yellow smoke into the atmosphere. It was an ugly, desperate place.

On September 23, 1935, two boys, playing at the foot of the steep embankment called Jackass Hill, spotted something among the weeds and went to investigate. A moment later, they were running, sprinting up the narrow path and away from the hideous sight they'd witnessed. At the top of the ridge, they ran into a man who stopped them in their tracks and demanded to know what they were up to.

"There's a man down there," one of the boys blurted, "And he hasn't got a head!"

The first police officers on the scene were Detectives Emil Musil and Orly May of Cleveland PD. They found not one, but two

headless corpses, as described in the police report dated
September 23, 1935:

"We found the bodies of two white men, both beheaded, lying in
the weeds; both bodies were naked except that one of them had
socks on. After an extensive search, the heads of both men were
found buried in separate places, one about 20 feet away from one
of the bodies and the other head was buried about 75 feet away
from the other body. Both men's penises had been severed from
their bodies and were found near one of the heads. We also found
an old blue coat; light cap and a blood stained union suit. Nearby
was a metal bucket containing a small quantity of oil and a torch. It
was apparent that oil, acid or some chemical was poured over one
of the bodies as it was burnt to quite an extent; it was also evident
that both bodies had been there several days as they had started to
decompose."

The autopsy added some additional information. Victim One was
estimated to be 40 to 45 years old and had been dead for 7 to 10
days. He'd been decapitated while still alive and his skin had been
scorched post-mortem. Advanced decomposition prevented the
taking of fingerprints.

Victim Two was younger, perhaps in his twenties, and had been
dead 2-3 days. He too had been killed by decapitation, and there
were rope burns on his wrists, leading the coroner to believe that
he'd been emasculated while still alive. In this case, an
identification was possible. He was Edward A. Andrassy, a resident
of Cleveland, 28 years old at the time of his death.

The police began looking into Andrassy's background and found
no shortage of people who might have wanted him dead. Born to
Hungarian immigrants from a once aristocratic family, the
handsome, dark-haired man had a somewhat insalubrious
reputation. His police record showed that he'd spent several terms
in the Warrensville Workhouse, once on a concealed weapons
charge, on numerous occasions for public intoxication. Detectives
who'd had dealings with him in the past described him as a "snotty
punk."

Andrassy's mother told police that two months earlier a middle-
aged man had arrived at their house threatening to kill Edward for
"paying attentions to his wife." His father said Andrassy associated
with "people of questionable character."

The police learned that Andrassy had once committed sodomy on
a woman while posing as a doctor. They also found out that he was
bisexual, that he dealt in pornographic literature and that he was a
habitual marijuana smoker. Andrassy's long list of enemies
included several men whose wives he'd seduced, as well as local
Italian and Oriental gangsters. In short, few people would have
made a more likely candidate for murder than Edward Andrassy.

After a few days of investigation, the police were ready to
disregard any gang-related connections. They believed that the
crimes related to Andrassy's philandering, that the victims were
known to each other and that they'd been killed by the same
person. There was, of course, another possibility - that the
murders were random and had been committed by a homicidal
maniac. However, the police weren't prepared to entertain that

possibility, even though there had been another murder, earlier in the year, which bore striking similarities to the double homicide.

In that instance, the lower half of a woman's torso had washed up on the shore of Lake Erie near the Euclid Beach amusement park. The legs had been severed at the knees and the odd coloration of the skin suggested that the body had been scorched after death. Two weeks later, the upper portion of the woman's torso washed up some 30 miles away. The rest of the corpse was never found and the victim was never identified, although the press dubbed her, "The Lady of the Lake."

By November 1935, the homicide investigation had gone cold and the detectives had moved on to fresher cases (of which there were many in Depression-era Cleveland). A mayoral election was held that month and Republican candidate Harold Burton was swept into office on a promise to clean up the city and rehabilitate its police force. Burton's first act was to appoint Eliot Ness, a young crime fighter who would later achieve fame for his role in bringing down Al Capone.

Ness got to work immediately, launching a major offensive against the city's mobsters. He also introduced steps to tackle police corruption and to upgrade the caliber of officers in the Cleveland PD. As news of Ness' victories dominated the headlines, Clevelanders had every reason to believe that they were winning the battle against crime. They could have had no inkling that their city was about to become embroiled in one of the most notorious murder sagas in its history.

On the bitterly cold Sunday of January 26, 1936, police received a report of dismembered bodies parts lying against a wall on East 21st Place. Responding to the call, officers found parts of a female body in a half-bushel basket, other parts wrapped in burlap sacks.

The detectives transported the remains (the lower half of a torso, both thighs and the upper right chest with the right arm attached) to the coroner. He determined that the woman had been dead between two and four days, that the cuts had been made with a very sharp instrument and that the perpetrator was experienced at cutting flesh.

Meanwhile, the right hand was fingerprinted and sent to the police department Bertillon division. They came back with the identity of the murdered woman soon after. Florence Saudy Polillo was a stout 42-year-old with reddish hair and a fair complexion. She had been arrested a number of times for prostitution which was why her fingerprints were on file.

Looking into Polillo's background detectives found a sad tale of a woman whose life had been destroyed by drink. Flo was described as friendly and kind when sober, but aggressive and combative when intoxicated. She'd been married once, but the marriage had ended after six years, due to her heavy drinking. After that, she'd drifted from one abusive relationship to another. Eventually, she'd resorted to prostitution to earn a living. By the time of her death, her closest associates were pimps, whorehouse madams, prostitutes, bootleggers, and drug addicts – the dregs of society. Still, it appeared that she was universally liked. No one had any idea who might have wanted her dead.

On February 7, 1936, the rest of Flo's body, with the exception of her head, was found lying against a fence behind a derelict building. The cold weather had preserved the remains in remarkably good condition, allowing the coroner, Dr. Pearse, to make a chilling discovery. Flo Polillo had been alive when her head had been severed.

As in the case of Edward Andrassy and his unidentified companion, the investigation into Flo Polillo's murder soon hit a wall. There were simply no clues to go on and, while some on the force felt that four decapitation deaths within 18 months was highly unusual, no one suspected that a serial killer might be at work. Not yet.

On Friday, June 5, 1936, on the eve of the Republican National Convention, which was being hosted in Cleveland, two young boys on their way to do some fishing took a shortcut through Kingsbury Run. As they passed an area of dense bush, they saw a pair of pants rolled up into a bundle. Curious at what the bundle might contain, they began poking at it with a fishing pole. To their horror, a man's head rolled out onto the path. Terrified, the boys ran back home and waited until their mother arrived to call the police.

Later that afternoon, the police found the head and launched a search for the man's body. The naked, headless corpse was found the next morning, concealed in bushes outside the Nickel Plate police station. It was as if it had been left there to taunt the authorities.

The victim had been a tall, slender man with a handsome face, estimated to be in his mid-twenties. He had a number of distinctive tattoos on his body and was thought perhaps to be a sailor. He was certainly not a hobo, as he was clean-shaven and well nourished. The clothes found nearby were clean and of good quality. Given the absence of blood at the crime scene, the police believed that he'd been killed somewhere else before being dumped in Kingsbury Run.

But it was the nature of the wounds than concerned Coroner Pearse. Once again it appeared that the man had been killed by decapitation, just like Flo Polillo, just like Edward Andrassy and his unidentified companion, perhaps even like "The Lady of The Lake." Decapitation is a most unusual way to commit murder and yet, here were four, maybe five, such crimes within two years.

Pearse took his findings to Elliot Ness, and although Ness saw his priorities elsewhere, and had no intention of becoming personally involved in the murder investigation, he was alarmed enough to convene a meeting of senior detectives.

On the Sunday before the Republican Convention, he called in the head of the Homicide Division, Sergeant James Hogan, and the head of the crime lab, Lieutenant David Cowles. Ness expressed the belief (and Cowles agreed) that the five murders were the work of the same man. Hogan was somewhat more circumspect but eventually agreed to conduct inquiries based on that premise. He got to work immediately, launching a massive, but ultimately fruitless, operation to identify the latest victim, the so-called "Tattooed Man."

Meanwhile, the Republican Convention went off without a hitch and was followed in short order by the equally successful Great Lakes Expo. Cleveland and the country in general were on the up, the Depression banished and a brighter future ahead.

Things were not looking as bright for the murder investigation, though. Not only had Cleveland PD failed in their efforts to identify the Tattooed Man, but on July 22, 1936, a call came in about another murder. A teenaged girl had stumbled upon the headless corpse of a white male, near a hobo camp.

The naked corpse was found lying on its stomach, the head some fifteen feet from the body. The blood that had seeped into the ground suggested that he'd been killed where he lay. The coroner's report noted that the man had been dead for about two months. Rodents, maggots, and the process of decomposition had removed much of the internal viscera, but the expert decapitation marked this out as the work of the same killer.

Normally, the murder of an unnamed homeless man would attract little, if any, media attention. However, the press had caught the whiff of a sensational story, and while Elliot Ness' continuing campaign against organized crime still dominated the front page, all three of Cleveland's newspapers carried stories about a psychopathic maniac on the loose in the city. By mid-September, with the discovery of yet another headless corpse, there would be only one story in town.

On September 10, a hobo sitting near a stagnant pool on the corner of East 37th Street spotted something in the water. On closer inspection, it proved to be two halves of a human torso.

The police were called and immediately launched a search for the rest of the body. Finding nothing in the nearby brush they ordered the pool dragged and eventually recovered two lower legs and the right thigh. However, for identification purposes, it was the head and hands they needed. As a crowd gathered to watch proceedings, the search went on well into the night.

Meanwhile, confirmation came from the coroner that this victim had been killed in the same way as the others, by expert decapitation. And then the afternoon papers hit the streets and a sense of hysteria descended on the city of Cleveland as the nameless killer was given a chilling persona: The Mad Butcher of Kingsbury Run.

The next morning, with the 'Mad Butcher' still dominating the front pages, and the crowd of spectators swelled to hundreds, divers descended into the murky depths of the pool to search for the head and hands. When this proved unsuccessful, the Coast Guard was called in with their specialist equipment. Still they turned up nothing.

Eliot Ness had hoped to avoid becoming personally involved in the investigation, but with the growing list of victims and the first hints of criticism against him and his police force filtering into the press, he knew he had to do something. After interviewing several of the detectives working the case, he personally took charge.

Ness' first action was to assign twenty detectives to work exclusively on the case. Then he ordered the hobo population of Kingsbury Run cleaned out and urged the public to come forward with information. This last move proved more of a hindrance than a help to the police. They were soon inundated with calls. It seemed that every person in Cleveland had a theory as to who the 'Mad Butcher' might be. Anyone who kept odd hours or carried a knife appeared to be fair game.

A few days after the latest murder, the Cleveland News put up a $100 reward, a substantial sum in those days. Meanwhile, the police tried some unorthodox methods in their efforts to catch the killer. Detectives staked out Kingsbury Run by dressing as hobos and hiding in the bushes. Others frequented gay bars and bathhouses, looking for leads on homosexual men with sadistic tendencies.

Wild stories about the killer's identity abounded, many of them driven by the press. One popular theory was that he was a wealthy doctor who killed for sport, targeting people from the lower classes. Another held that he was a religious zealot, another that he was a Jekyll and Hyde type character who killed whenever his bloodlust overwhelmed him.

That happened again on February 23, 1937, when the upper torso of a woman was found on the beach at 156th Street, in almost the exact location where body parts from the Lady of the Lake had been found in 1934. Like the others, this victim had been decapitated. Her arms had also been amputated and the torso bisected. More than two months later, the lower portion of the torso would be found floating off East 30th Street, close to the mouth of the Cuyahoga River.

Victim Seven was the first to be seen by the newly elected Coroner Samuel Gerber. He determined that the woman had been dead two to four days and in the water no longer than three. She was between 25 and 35 years old and weighed approximately 100 to 120 pounds. The legs and arms had been removed with the murderer's usual skill, but the bisection of the torso showed several hesitation marks. Unlike in the other victims, decapitation was post-mortem. And the killer had added a bizarre touch. He had inserted a pants pocket inside the woman's rectum.

In the wake of this latest murder, Eliot Ness made an urgent plea to the newspapers, urging them to tone down the sensationalist nature of their reporting about the case. To back up his argument, Ness produced a number of opinions he'd commissioned from various psychiatrists. The consensus was that the frenzy whipped up by lurid front-page headlines was feeding the warped ego of the Butcher, encouraging him to kill again. For the most part, the newspaper editors complied, but it did nothing to slow the killer.

On June 6, 1937, a teenager named Russell Lawer made a gruesome discovery under the Lorain-Carnegie Bridge - skeletal remains in a rotting burlap bag.

The victim was an African American woman of very small stature. A newspaper found along with the body suggested that she'd been dead for approximately a year. The arms and legs were missing, but the skull was intact and showed extensive dental work. It was impossible to tell how the victim had died, but there was considerable hacking around the 3rd, 4th, and 5th cervical vertebrae. The body had also been treated with quicklime.

A month after the discovery of the latest body, the Mad Butcher struck again, returning to his old killing ground of Kingsbury Run. On July 6, 1937, the upper portion of a man's torso, plus his two thighs, were found floating in the Cuyahoga River near the Run. Over the next week, other body parts surfaced, all except the head, which was never found.

Like most of the others, Victim Nine went unidentified. However, the decapitation murder bore the clear signature of the Mad Butcher. He'd added a new twist, though - all of the internal organs, including the heart, had been removed, apparently by an expert hand. So expert, in fact, that the coroner, Dr. Gerber, believed that the Mad Butcher might be a medical professional.

This had been suggested before, leading the police to focus their investigation heavily on doctors, male nurses and medical students. They'd even honed in on a likely suspect - Dr. Frank E. Sweeney. A physically powerful man who had grown up in the Kingsbury Run area, Sweeney had a serious drinking problem, which had cost him both his marriage and his surgical residency at St. Alexis Hospital. He was known to become violent when he drank and was also rumored to be bisexual. However, the police had abandoned Sweeney as a suspect in 1937 when it emerged that he was frequently out of town when the victims were discovered.

Now, though, a new piece of evidence came to light, one that put Frank Sweeney right back in the frame. In mid-March 1938, a report reached Lieutenant David Cowles of a severed leg that had been discovered by a dog. The incident had occurred in Sandusky, and that rang a bell with Cowles. Sandusky was where Dr. Sweeney had been staying at the time of most of the murders.

Cowles immediately set off for the town, where he discovered that Sweeney had voluntarily admitted himself to the VA hospital on several occasions, to receive treatment for his alcoholism. Some of these visits coincided with the Mad Butcher murders and thus seemed to provide Sweeney with a perfect alibi.

However, on closer investigation, Cowles learned that this was not necessarily the case. Patients who checked themselves into the hospital could pretty much come and go as they pleased. It would have been quite easy for Sweeney to leave the hospital, travel by car or train to Cleveland, commit a murder and return to the hospital without his absence being noticed.

Cowles also leaned that the Ohio Penitentiary Honor Farm shared some facilities with the veterans' hospital and that one of the inmates at the prison, a convicted burglar named Alex Archaki, was a close associate of Sweeney. Archaki, it seemed, kept Sweeney supplied with booze during his stays at Sandusky, while the good doctor reciprocated by writing prescriptions for barbiturates and other drugs. However, their arrangement didn't prevent Archaki from admitting to Cowles that he was convinced Sweeney was The Mad Butcher. According to Archaki, Sweeney's various absences from the hospital always seemed to coincide with a new victim turning up.

Cowles returned to Cleveland energized by his findings. As it turned out, the severed leg found by the dog was the result of legitimate surgery and not the work of The Mad Butcher. But at least Cowles had what he felt was a viable suspect. He began a discreet investigation, which only strengthened his belief that Dr. Sweeney was the Mad Butcher.

Sweeney was born, raised and spent most of his life in the Kingsbury Run area. He was a large and powerful man, enabling him to carry Edward Andrassy and his unidentified companion down the treacherous embankment of Jackass Hill. He possessed the medical know-how to carry out the expert decapitations and dismemberments of the victims. He was allegedly bisexual which might explain why he chose both male and female victims. Moreover, the timing of the first murder (the Lady of the Lake) coincided with a particular low point in Sweeney's life, the breakdown of his marriage. Might that have triggered his murderous campaign?

While Cowles pondered that question, the next victim turned up. On April 8, 1938, a woman's leg was fished out of the Cuyahoga River, followed over the next month by other body parts.

And the hue and cry over that discovery had barely died down when there was another gruesome find, this time at a dump on East 9th Street. The female body was wrapped in rags and brown paper, the head and hands uncharacteristically, found nearby. Then, as the police scoured the area for evidence, a bystander alerted them to more bones. This victim was a man aged between 30 and 40, dead for at least 3 months. The female was of a similar age but had been killed at a later date.

But were they victims of the Mad Butcher? The police didn't think so. They believed that the bodies had been left there, perhaps by medical students, as a prank. An autopsy didn't help in clearing up the mystery.

Regardless of what the police believed, public perception was that these two were the latest victims of the Mad Butcher. Political pressure on Ness and the police was cranked up to a whole new level. They had to be shown to be doing something to end the slaughter. After conferring with Mayor Burton and key members of the police department, Ness came to a decision, a bad miscalculation as it turned out.

On the night of August 18, 1938, two days after the bodies were found at the dump, Ness led a huge midnight raid on the city's shantytowns, chasing down and capturing terrified vagrants, fingerprinted them and carting them off to the workhouse. Police Officers then searched the rubble for evidence before setting the shacks ablaze.

The event caused a public outcry, with the police accused of victimizing the helpless and downtrodden rather than focusing their attention on catching the killer. Criticism of Ness and his department was scathing, with the press quick to point out that their long-running investigation had delivered up not one arrest, not one viable suspect.

Perhaps stung by these accusations, Ness made another crucial, but flawed, decision. He decided to bring in his main suspect for questioning. Given more time, Ness would probably have preferred to gather more evidence against Dr. Frank Sweeney before showing his hand. The doctor looked like a strong suspect, but whatever evidence they had against him was purely circumstantial.

Sweeney had, in fact, been under police surveillance for some time, but he seemed to be aware that he was being followed and appeared to enjoy teasing and taunting his pursuers. When he was asked to attend a police interrogation he readily agreed. He seemed amused at the prospect.

But despite Sweeney's apparent willingness to cooperate, the police had to proceed with the utmost discretion. The doctor was a first cousin to Ohio Congressman Martin L. Sweeney, an outspoken critic of Eliot Ness and the Cleveland PD. The last thing Ness needed was accusations that their interrogation of Sweeney was some kind of petty, politically motivated revenge. It was for this reason that the interrogation was conducted in secret, and not at police headquarters, but in a suite at the Cleveland Hotel.

The interrogation team consisted of four men: Eliot Ness, Lieutenant David Cowles, Dr. Royal Grossman (the court psychiatrist), and Dr. Leonard Keeler. Keeler was one of the inventors of the polygraph and Ness had brought him in from Chicago, specifically to oversee the lie detector test.

The initial round of questioning was carried out by Cowles and Grossman, but it was pretty obvious from the start that Sweeney was toying with them. He seemed mildly amused by the whole process, cracking jokes, and providing deliberately vague answers. When Keeler was finally ready, the polygraph equipment was wheeled in and the sensors fitted to Sweeney. Only Ness stayed behind as Keeler administered the polygraph.

After the usual innocuous questions to calibrate the machinery, Keeler got down to business, putting the questions that Cowles had prepared for him, "Have you ever met Edward Andrassy? Did you kill Edward Andrassy? Have you ever met Florence Polillo? Did you kill Florence Polillo?" Sweeney answered in the negative to each of these inquiries.

When the session concluded, Keeler asked Sweeney to stay behind while he and Ness left the room and joined Cowles and Grossman.

"Looks like he's your guy," Keeler said confidently.

"What do you think?" Ness asked Grossman, the psychiatrist.

"I believe we have a classic psychopath here with the likelihood of some schizophrenia."

Ness agreed but wanted Dr. Keeler to test Sweeney again just to be sure. The second round of testing, as well as the third, confirmed the earlier result, leaving the interrogation team convinced that Sweeney was The Mad Butcher. And yet, with only the polygraph and circumstantial evidence against Sweeney, Ness knew that he'd never get a conviction. The doctor walked away from the Cleveland Hotel a free man.

Ness was now in a quandary, a killer walking loose in the community and not much the police could do about it. He could, of course, keep Sweeney under surveillance, but the doctor had already proven adept at playing that game and giving his pursuers the slip. How long before he killed again?

As it turned out, Sweeney did have another surprise to offer, but it was not one that the police would ever have expected. Two days after the interrogation, he voluntarily admitted himself to the Sandusky VA Hospital. He would remain institutionalized, of his own accord, until his death in 1965.

Various theories exist as to why Sweeney committed himself and remained effectively a prisoner for the rest of his life. One is that Congressman Martin L. Sweeney struck some kind of deal with Ness. Another is that Sweeney's sisters convinced him to do so in order to spare their family the humiliation that an arrest and eventual trial would cause. Whatever the reason, the Kingsbury Run murders came to an abrupt end once Dr. Frank Sweeney was safely locked away.

The Monster Of Florence

Barbara Locci was a figure of scandal in Lastra a Signa, Italy. The married 32-year-old was known locally for her promiscuity, a trait that had earned her the nickname "Queen Bee." On the evening of August 21, 1968, Barbara was returning from a movie theater with her latest lover, Antonio Lo Bianco. With them, asleep in the backseat of the car, was Barbara's young son, Natalino. The night was somewhat cloudy and as they passed a local cemetery, Antonio suggested that they take advantage of the darkness and stop for a quick sexual liaison. Since her son was asleep, Barbara readily agreed. Antonio brought the car to a halt in the shadow of some trees and began unbuttoning Barbara's blouse. But he'd barely got started when a man emerged from the darkness. Before either of them could react, the man raised a gun and began firing, killing them both. He then pulled Natalino from the car and carried him away.

Sometime later that night, a local farmer was roused from sleep by someone knocking at his front door. When he opened the door, the young boy was standing there, tears running down his face. "My mother and my uncle are dead," the child cried. The farmer immediately called the police.

Investigators soon descended on the crime scene, where they found a bullet-riddled white Alfa Romeo, the victims slumped in the front seat. Eight .22-caliber shell casings lay beside the vehicle. A check on the vehicle's registration revealed that it belonged to Antonio Lo Bianco. His companion, investigators learned by questioning the boy, was Barbara Locci.

At around six o'clock the following morning, a police car was dispatched to the home that Barbara shared with her husband, Stefano Mele. As investigators approached the front door, it abruptly opened, and Mele stepped out, carrying a suitcase. He appeared to be in a hurry, immediately rousing police suspicions. Those suspicions hardened when he showed little reaction to the news of his wife's murder. The officers asked him to accompany them to police headquarters. Mele reluctantly agreed.

Once at the stationhouse, Mele was asked who he thought might have killed his wife. He gave the officers a catalog of names, including Carmelo Cutrona and the Vinci brothers - Giovanni, Salvatore, and Francesco. All of them, he said had been Barbara's lovers. Asked about his whereabouts at the time of the murders, Mele said he'd been at home, having gone to bed early, as he was feeling unwell. He was then released but told to return the next day.

The following day, August 23, 1968, Mele returned as instructed. This time, though, he had a surprise for the investigators. No sooner had they started interrogating him than he suddenly confessed to the double homicide. According to Mele, on the night of the murder, he'd sat up waiting for his wife until 11:20 p.m. When she hadn't returned he had gone looking for her. On reaching the town square of Lastra a Signa, he encountered Salvatore Vinci, who told him that Barbara was at the movies with Antonio Lo Bianco. Vinci had scolded him for allowing his wife to cheat on him. He had shown Mele a small pistol that he had with him and told him he should put a stop to it. The two of them then drove to the movie theater in Signa.

Seeing Lo Bianco's Alfa Romeo parked outside, they waited until they saw Lo Bianco and Barbara exit. Barbara was carrying Natalino in her arms. Mele and Vinci got into the car and followed them to the cemetery. Then, as Lo Bianco and Barbara started kissing, Vinci handed him the pistol. Mele got out of the car and walked towards Lo Bianco's vehicle, firing until the gun was empty. His son was asleep in the backseat throughout the hail of gunfire but woke immediately afterward. Mele then returned to Vinci's car and the two men drove to the Signa Bridge where they disposed of the gun. After that Vinci dropped him at home.

There were a number of problems with Mele's story, particularly relating to his son. Surely if the boy had seen him, he'd have recognized his own father? And were the police really to believe that Mele had fled the scene leaving Natalino alone with the bloody corpse of his mother? Even if he had done so, how had the boy ended up at the farmhouse? Nonetheless, the police seemed prepared to accept Mele's version of events and he was placed under arrest.

The following day, August 24, 1968, the police began their search for the murder weapon. Unable to locate it, they returned to question Mele further. Now, he changed his story. First, he said that the weapon hadn't been thrown from the bridge and that Salvatore Vinci still had it. Then, he recanted his entire confession, insisting that Salvatore's brother, Francesco Vinci, had killed Barbara.

This new version of events cut little ice with the authorities. Mele remained incarcerated until his trial two years later. He was found guilty and sentenced to 14 years in prison, the sentence mitigated by temporary insanity.

Six years after the murders of Barbara Locci and Antonio Lo
Bianco, the police received a call about another brutal double
homicide, when the bodies of 18-year-old Stefania Pettini and 19-
year-old Pasquale Gentilcore were discovered in a parked car on
September 14, 1974.

Investigators rushed to the scene at Borgo San Lorenzo, just north
of Florence.
They found a Fiat 127, the half-naked body of a young man
slumped at the wheel, the victim of numerous gunshot wounds. At
the rear of the car lay the nude body of a young woman,
grotesquely posed. Her arms and legs were in a spread-eagle
position and a vine branch had been inserted into her vagina. It
appeared that she'd been stabbed to death.

The autopsy filled in the missing details. Both victims had been
shot numerous times with a small-caliber pistol, a .22 Beretta
according to the ballistics report. The bullets were of a distinctive
Winchester type, manufactured in Australia during the 1950s. The
male victim had been shot five times, the female three. Her death
was the result of 96 stab wounds, delivered by a long-bladed knife.

As the police investigation continued three suspects emerged: 53-
year-old Bruno Mocali, a self-proclaimed faith healer; Guido
Giovannini, a peeping tom who had been seen spying on couples in
the area where the murder took place; and Giuseppe Francini, a
mentally unstable man who had walked into a police station and
confessed to the killings. However, there was no evidence linking
any of the men to the crime, and with no leads or suspects to
pursue, the case went cold.

Seven years passed with no progress in the Borgo San Lorenzo
murders. Then, on Saturday, June 6, 1981, a police sergeant out for

a walk with his young son, chanced upon a copper-colored Fiat Ritmo parked at the side of a road. A woman's handbag was lying next to the driver's door, its contents scattered on the ground. His curiosity aroused, the sergeant decided to investigate. As he approached the vehicle, he noticed that the driver's side window had been smashed. Sitting at the wheel was the body of a young man whose throat appeared to have been slashed. The sergeant immediately went to report the crime.

As investigators arrived at the crime scene, they soon discovered the body of a female victim lying at the bottom of a steep bank, some 20 yards away. Her legs were splayed, her T-shirt and jeans were slashed. It was immediately obvious that she'd suffered horrendous wounds to her lower abdomen and the investigators realized to their horror that her vagina had been crudely removed.

An autopsy revealed that both victims had died from multiple gunshots. The man had also been stabbed three times, twice in the neck and once in the chest. The excision of the girl's vagina had been performed with an extremely sharp instrument, possibly a scalpel.

An identification of the victims came soon after. They were 21-year-old Carmela De Nuccio and her 30-year-old lover, Giovanni Foggi. Then came the ballistics report and with it a shocking revelation. The weapon that had killed De Nuccio and Foggi was the same one that had been used in the Borgo San Lorenzo murders, seven years before. The police were hunting a serial killer.

And they soon had a suspect in custody. Enzo Spalletti was known locally as a voyeur and his red Ford had been seen close to the scene on the night of the murder. Even more incriminating was the fact that Spalletti had told his wife about two bodies discovered in a copper-colored Fiat Ritmo, before those details had been reported in the press. He was quickly charged with the crime and locked up pending trial. However, he'd soon be proven innocent.

The killer had waited seven years between his last two crimes. This time, he'd wait less than five months. On Oct. 23, 1981, 24-year-old Susanna Cambi and her 26-year-old boyfriend, Stefano Baldi, parked at a scenic outlook near Calenzano, just north of Florence. Later that evening, another couple discovered their bullet-ridden and mutilated corpses.

Investigators arriving at the scene found a young man lying next to a Volkswagen motor vehicle. He was half-naked and appeared to have been shot and stabbed numerous times. A female victim lay on the opposite side of the car. She too had been shot and stabbed, but her killer hadn't stopped there, as with Carmella De Nuccio, he'd removed her vagina.

A pathologist determined that the killer had stood in front of the vehicle and shot both victims through the windshield. He'd then attacked them with a knife while they were still alive. The excision of the vagina had again been performed with an extremely sharp instrument. He'd taken less care this time, cutting away a large section of flesh, lacerating the abdominal wall and leaving the intestines exposed. Ballistics reports linked these murders to the others.

In the wake of the latest murders, the police decided to go public with the news that a serial killer was at work in the area. Their intention was to warn young couples of the dangers of parking in isolated areas. But they also hoped that the news might prompt members of the public to come forward with any information they might have. In the event, all they achieved was to cause a panic, especially as the media had now come up with a terrifying name for the unknown perpetrator. They called him Il Mostro – The Monster.

On June 19, 1982, the Monster struck again, this time near Montespertoli, southwest of Florence. Paolo Mainardi, 22, and his girlfriend, 20-year-old Antonella Migliorini, were making out in a parked car near the Via Nuova Virgilio provincial roadway when a man stepped from cover and began firing at them. Antonella died almost immediately. Paolo, although seriously injured, was able to start the car, turn on the headlights, and reverse.

Unfortunately, the car ended up in a ditch. The killer then closed in and emptied his pistol into the two victims, before turning off the car's ignition and tossing the keys into the bushes. Perhaps because of traffic in the area, he performed no post-mortem mutilations, instead fleeing the scene, leaving Paolo Mainardi mortally wounded, but still breathing.

The crime scene was discovered the following morning, by which time Paolo had lost consciousness. He was rushed to hospital but died there a few hours later, making him Il Mostro's tenth victim.

Later that morning, the assistant district attorney, Silvia Della Monica, convened a press conference in her office and asked for assistance from the media in spreading some misinformation. She asked them to report that Paolo Mainardi had given a description of the killer before he died. All of the reporters agreed, and the information was reported in the afternoon papers.

The assistant DA's plan was to make to killer nervous, hoping to panic him into a mistake. To an extent, it worked. That same day,

one of the paramedics who had accompanied Paolo Mainardi to
the hospital received a call from a person claiming to be the killer.
He wanted to know what Paolo had told the police.

A few days after the latest murders, a police sergeant who had
worked the Locci / Lo Bianco case, began to wonder if that case
might be connected to the current series. He called for the
ballistics records and compared them to those from the later
crimes. It was a match. The pistol used to kill Locci and Lo Bianco
in 1968 was the same one used in the other murders.

On Sept. 9, 1983, a year after the last double murder, the Monster
killed again, although this time he broke his pattern by murdering
two male victims. Horst Meyer and Uwe Rusch Sens, both 24, were
German tourists on a camping holiday in Italy. The two young men
were shot to death while sleeping in a Volkswagen camper parked
at Galluzzo, some 19 miles south of Florence. The crimes were not
linked to Il Mostro until ballistics tests provided a match.
Investigators speculated that the killer might have mistaken one of
the victims, who had long blonde hair, for a woman.

The police had meanwhile begun to pick up a number of
commonalities to the killings. Aside from the obvious ballistic
connection, most of the shootings had happened on a Saturday and
nearly all of the victims had been at a nightclub on the nights they
died. The only exceptions were Barbara Locci and Antonio Lo
Bianco, who been at a movie. Was it possible that the killer had
tracked his victims from these places of entertainment?

While the police puzzled over that conundrum they were
presented with an unusual theory. Massimo Introvigne, a religious
historian, suggested to the investigators that the crimes might
have occult connections. He explained that Florence had a long

tradition of sorcery and that the ritual nature of the murders suggested that occultists were involved. Outlandish though this theory seemed, the investigators were quite willing to entertain it, especially given the mutilations carried out on the female victims.

The killer waited almost a year before he struck again on July 29, 1984, murdering a young couple in Vicchio di Mugello, just north of Florence. The victims were Claudio Stefanacci, 21, and his 18-year-old girlfriend Pia Gilda Rontini. Claudio's body was found on the backseat of his car wearing only underpants and a vest. Not far from the vehicle, concealed behind some bushes, lay the naked body of Pia Rontini. She'd been posed in a spread eagle position, and her genitals had been hacked away. The killer had also cut off her left breast and inflicted over 100 slash wounds on her body. An autopsy showed that both victims had been shot before being stabbed.

There were no fingerprints left at the scene and no other clues. After nearly two decades hunting the killer, the police had to admit that they were no closer to catching Il Mostro than in 1968. All they could do was wait and hope that next time, he'd make a mistake.

Another year would pass before the beast struck again, emerging from the shadows on September 8, 1985, to murder a vacationing French couple, 25-year-old Jean-Michel Kraveichvili and 36-year-old Nadine Mauriot. The victims had been camping at San Casciano, just outside of Florence. Nadine's body was discovered inside a tent, three bullets lodged in her skull, a forth in her throat. The male victim, Jean-Michelle, had also been shot four times. However, he was found some 30 yards away. It appeared that he'd tried to escape the attacker but had been overtaken and stabbed to death. The killer had then returned to the tent to work on the woman's corpse, removing her vagina and left breast.

On the day following the latest murders, an envelope was delivered to assistant DA Silvia Della Monica at the public prosecutor's office. Inside was a small plastic bag containing a cube of flesh from Nadine Mauriot's breast.

The Kraveichvili / Mauriot double homicide was the last known to have been committed by the Monster of Florence. Over the next eight years, investigators continued working the case, questioning more than 100,000 people in the hope of gaining a lead. Their inquiries led them to focus on Pietro Pacciani, a 68-year-old semi-literate farmer. Pacciani had served prison time in 1951 for the murder of a traveling salesman, whom he had caught in bed with his fiancé. Released from prison after serving 13 years, Pacciani married and fathered two daughters. He did prison time again in 1987 and in 1991, first for assaulting his wife, then for sexually molesting his two young daughters.

Pacciani was believed to be involved in an occult group with three other men, Mario Vanni, Giovanni Faggi and Giancarlo Lotti, all of whom were known locally as peeping toms and perverts. This unholy quartet was reputed to have taken part in black masses, using female body parts in the ceremonies. An unnamed doctor was said to preside over these satanic rites, which supposedly took place at a house in San Caciano.

Despite the rather tenuous nature of the evidence against him, Pacciani was arrested on January 17, 1993. His trial began almost a year later in November 1994 and despite his protestations of innocence, he was found guilty on seven counts of murder.

Pacciani was sentenced to life in prison. However, the conviction was always vulnerable to challenge and on February 13, 1996, an appeals court overturned it. Amidst a public outcry, 71-year-old Pietro Pacciani was set free. Just hours later, his fellow occultists Mario Vanni and Giancarlo Lotti were arrested for their involvement in the murders. They would ultimately be convicted and sentenced to life and 26 years respectively.

Pietro Pacciani, meanwhile, enjoyed very little of his new found liberty. On February 23, 1998, he was found lying face down on the floor of his home. Initially, his death appeared to have been the result of a heart attack. However, a post-mortem examination revealed a lethal combination of drugs in his system. Pacciani had been due to appear in court for a retrial of his case. The investigating magistrate firmly believed that he'd been silenced, lest he reveal the identity of the real Monster of Florence.

Jack the Ripper

By today's standards, Jack the Ripper is a pretty run-of-the-mill serial killer. The murderer of five women, all of them prostitutes, he'd barely make the headlines in an age of Bundy, Dahmer, and Chikatilo. Why then are we still so obsessed with the Ripper? Why, over a century since he committed his horrendous crimes, does he still command such morbid fascination?

Perhaps it is because the case is a classic murder mystery. A fiend emerges from the fog, taking victims at will, his bloodlust escalating with each crime. Then, after a finale of unspeakable violence, he vanishes, leaving us to ponder who he was and why he did it. It has all the elements of a perfect whodunit, except in this case there's no Sherlock Holmes or Hercule Poirot to point out the murderer for us.

The Ripper first announced his deadly presence on August 31, 1888. At around four o'clock on that chilly Friday morning, Charles Cross was walking along Whitechapel's Buck's Row when he saw something on the ground. It looked to him like a discarded tarpaulin, but as he drew closer, he realized that it was a woman lying on her back, her skirts lifted almost to her waist. Thinking that she was either drunk or the victim of an assault he went to her assistance, summoning help from another passerby. As they drew closer, though, they saw the awful wounds to her throat. They ran immediately to look for a policeman.

Cross and his companion had not yet returned when Police Constable John Neil found the body while walking his regular beat. By the light of his lantern, he could see that the woman's throat had been slashed from ear to ear. Neil squatted beside the corpse and felt her hands. They were cold, but her upper arms still retained some warmth, indicating that she hadn't been dead long. He then called to another policeman and told him to summon a doctor and an ambulance.

While Neil waited for the surgeon to arrive, he knocked at some of the houses and questioned the residents trying to find out if anyone had seen or heard anything. No one had. Soon, Dr. Rees Llewellyn arrived at the scene and examined the woman. He estimated that she'd been dead no longer than half an hour, the cause of death two deep slashes to the throat that had severed the windpipe and esophagus. The body was removed to the mortuary on Old Montague Street, where it was discovered that her abdomen had also been mutilated. Dr. Llewellyn was then called back for a more thorough examination.

One of the first things the doctor noticed was a bruise to the lower left jaw, suggesting perhaps that she'd been knocked out before being cut. The wound to the abdomen was deep and jagged, inflicted, according to the doctor, by a left-handed person wielding a long-bladed knife. Later, the doctor would revise his opinion about the killer being left-handed.

It was estimated that the woman had been lying on her back when she'd been killed. That would explain why there was relatively little blood at the scene, the majority of it having seeped into her clothes. Extrapolating on this theory, the police believed that the killer had knocked the woman out with a blow to the jaw, then laid her on the ground before slashing her throat. He'd then lifted her skirt and carried out his post-mortem mutilations to her abdomen.

Next, the police had to try to identify the victim, no easy task when all she had in her possession was a comb, a broken mirror, and a handkerchief. However, as word of the murder spread across Whitechapel, the police heard of a woman named "Polly," who was missing from her lodgings at 18 Thrawl Street. "Polly" turned out to be Mary Ann Nichols, age 42. Her father and her husband identified her the next day.

Polly had been married to William Nichols, a printer's machinist, but their marriage had broken down due to her drinking and she'd drifted into prostitution, selling herself on the streets for a pittance that was soon spent on booze in the nearest tavern. It was a pitiful life, brought to a brutal end.

The officer assigned to the investigation was Chief Inspector Frederick George Abberline, a veteran with 25 years on the force, most of them spent in the Whitechapel area. Abberline must have known instinctively that the case was going to be nigh on impossible to solve. He already had two unsolved prostitute murders on his books.

On Monday, August 6, 1888, a 39-year-old prostitute named Martha Tabram had been stabbed to death in George Yard, the killer inflicting 39 wounds to her body, neck and private parts with a long bladed knife, thought to be a bayonet.

Some months earlier, on April 2, 1888, 45-year-old prostitute Emma Smith was attacked at a spot just 100 yards from where Tabram would be found. Her head and face were badly battered and a blunt instrument had been forced into her vagina. Before she died, Smith said that the attack had been perpetrated by a group of men, who'd also robbed her.

Many residents of Whitechapel believed that these attacks, and the Polly Nicholls murder, were the work of the same man. This is highly unlikely. Smith was attacked by a group of men, and the motive appeared to be robbery. The other two were almost certainly carried out by a person working alone. Is it possible then that the same person who killed Polly Nicholls also killed Martha Tabram, that Tabram was, in fact, Jack the Ripper's first victim? Some Ripper experts believe so. Others do not.

In order to understand the Jack the Ripper murders, it is necessary to know something about the background against which they took place. London's East End, in Victorian England, was a teeming slum of some nine hundred thousand people, a place where sheep and cattle were herded through the narrow streets to the many slaughterhouses, where the thoroughfares were littered with blood and excrement and the air was thick with the stench of rotting garbage and liquid sewage. Most of the inhabitants lived in filthy tenement houses under terrible, crowded conditions. More than half of the children born into this squalor died before the age of five. Of those who survived, many were physically or mentally handicapped.

For the most part, the people living in the East End during this era were employed at menial work, although many were unemployed and many more subsisted through various criminal enterprises. For the East End's women, there was even less opportunity. Prostitution was one of the few reliable means through which they could earn a living. Police estimates put Whitechapel's prostitute population in 1888, at 1,200. That is aside from those women who took to occasional whoring to supplement their meager earnings.

In short, Whitechapel was an area known for poverty and crime, squalor and crowded tenements, narrow darkened streets and alleyways. The perfect hunting ground, in other words, for an enterprising serial killer.

The death of Polly Nicholls, recognized by most experts as the Ripper's first victim, caused great concern in the East End. It was not that the area's residents were unused to violent crime, but in their minds, the Tabram, Smith, and Nichols murders had been committed by the same man and, as there appeared very little motive to the crimes, the consensus was that the perpetrator must be some homicidal maniac.

A request was made to the Home Secretary, Henry Matthews, to offer a reward for the apprehension of the criminal, but Matthews refused, saying he had faith in the Metropolitan Police's ability to apprehend the killer.

And the police soon had a suspect. Shortly after the Nicholls murder, a story emerged about a man known locally as "Leather Apron," who habitually extorted money from prostitutes, and beat them if they refused to pay. He was described as being five-foot-four, heavyset with a particularly thick neck. His eyes were "small and glistening", his lips perpetually parted in a menacing grin, his hair black and closely cropped. He wore a small, black mustache and was always attired in a black, leather apron, hence his nickname.

But finding "Leather Apron," proved a challenge. Fearful of mob violence, the suspect had gone into hiding. He was soon ruled out of the investigation anyway, as the next murder victim turned up.

Annie Chapman, like Polly Nicholls, was an alcoholic prostitute. Known to her friends as "Dark Annie," Chapman had once been a respectable, married woman with three children. However, after one of her children died of meningitis, both she and her husband, John, took to drink, leading to the eventual breakdown of the marriage. Things got even worse when John died and Annie lost the small allowance that he had provided her. Suffering from depression and alcoholism, and left with no means of support, she had drifted into prostitution.

On Saturday, September 8, 1888, a slightly inebriated Annie was turned away from lodgings because she didn't have enough money to pay for a bed. She promised to return soon with the correct amount. Later that morning, her mutilated body was found in the backyard of 29 Hanbury Street, Spitalfields, just a few hundred yards away.

John Davis, an elderly carman who lived with his wife and three sons at 29 Hanbury, discovered Annie's body just after 6 a.m. He went immediately for help, returning with a constable.

Annie Chapman was found lying on her back, her legs drawn up, with the feet resting on the ground and the knees turned outwards. Her face was swollen with the tongue protruding between her front teeth. Her abdomen had been sliced open and the viscera pulled through the wound with the small intestines lying on the right side of the body above the right shoulder, yet still attached. Part of the stomach had been removed and lay on the ground above the left shoulder. The throat had been deeply slashed and there was a large quantity of blood on the ground.

Dr. George Bagster Phillips, the veteran police surgeon who conducted the examination, estimated that the victim had been dead approximately two hours. She'd been murdered where she was found and yet none of the 17 people living at 29 Hanbury (many with windows overlooking the murder scene) had heard anything. Dr. Phillips believed this was because she'd been strangled into unconsciousness before her throat was slashed.

Further testimony as to the brutality of the crime was provided by Dr. Phillips at the inquest. The murderer had grabbed Annie by the chin and slashed her throat deeply from left to right. He may have been trying to decapitate her and though he failed in this, the laceration was severe enough to cause death. The abdominal mutilations, were postmortem and described as follows:

"The abdomen had been entirely laid open; that the intestines, severed from their mesenteric attachments, had been lifted out of the body, and placed by the shoulder of the corpse; whilst from the pelvis the uterus and its appendages, with the upper portion of the vagina and the posterior two-thirds of the bladder, had been entirely removed. No trace of these parts could be found, and the incisions were cleanly cut, avoiding the rectum, and dividing the vagina low enough to avoid injury to the cervix uteri. Obviously, the work was that of an expert - of one, at least, who had such knowledge of anatomical or pathological examinations as to be enabled to secure the pelvic organs with one sweep of the knife."

Phillips went on to say that the operation had been performed for the purpose of harvesting the body parts. He expressed surprise that the cuts could have been done so expertly, in such a short time span. He stated that he, a surgeon of 23 years experience, would have needed fifteen minutes at least and, more likely, an hour.

Coroner Wynne E. Baxter agreed in his summation, stating that he believed the perpetrator to be someone with "considerable anatomical skill and knowledge."

The Annie Chapman murder investigation was assigned to Inspector Joseph Chandler of the Metropolitan Police's H Division. However, Inspector Abberline, who was in charge of the Polly Nichols murder, was instructed to assist, even though it fell outside his jurisdiction. The top brass at the Met clearly believed that the same man had committed both murders.

As in the Nicholls murder, the Chapman investigation soon became bogged down for lack of evidence. The killer had taken considerable risk, committing the crime in daylight, right across the road from the busy Spitalfields market. And yet there were no concrete leads, no idea as to a motive or a suspect.

The police were not entirely without clues, though – three important witnesses came forward, and one of them had almost certainly caught a glimpse of the murderer. The first witness, John Richardson, was the son of Mrs. Amelia Richardson, who owned 29 Hanbury.

On the morning of the murder, between 4:45 and 4:50, he had visited the house in order to check the locks on the cellar. It was just getting light and he could see that the locks hadn't been tampered with, so he sat down to cut a strip of leather from his boot, as it was hurting his foot. He saw no one in the yard, which means that Annie Chapman hadn't been killed yet.

"I could not have failed to notice the deceased had she been lying there then," he said at the inquest.

Another witness, Albert Cadosch, lived next door to 29 Hanbury Street. He testified that at around 5:20 a.m., he heard a woman's voice speak a single word "No!"

But the most important witness was Mrs. Elizabeth Long. She said that she passed by 29 Hanbury Street on her way to Spitalfields market at 5:30. She saw a man and a woman talking in the yard, the woman facing her, the man with his back to her. She later identified Annie Chapman as the woman she'd seen.

The murder of Annie Chapman coming so close on the brutal killings of Polly Nicholls and Martha Tabram cast a pall of fear and suspicion over the East End. Sensing an upswing in anti-Semitic sentiment, some local businessmen got together to form the Mile

End Vigilance Committee, a sort of neighborhood watch, under the leadership of local building contractor, George Lusk. Meanwhile, Samuel Montagu, the Jewish Member of Parliament for Whitechapel, offered a reward for the capture of the killer.

Yet, even with a homicidal maniac on the loose, it didn't take long for Whitechapel's bawdy nightlife to return to its usual raucous level. Too many people's livelihoods depended on it.

On Tuesday, September 11, a few days after the murder of Annie Chapman, John Pizer, the infamous "Leather Apron," was finally arrested. However, the police already knew that Pizer wasn't the Whitechapel murderer. He didn't match the description of the man Elizabeth Long had seen with Chapman, neither did he possess the anatomical knowledge and surgical skill of the killer. Besides, Pizer was able to provide solid alibis for each of the murders. A rather unsavory character he may have been, but Pizer wasn't the man they sought. He was soon released.

A number of other arrests followed. In the main, these were drunks who shot their mouths off about the murders while under the influence. Few of them were retained for very long after it was discovered that they lacked the surgical skill required to have carried out the mutilations on Annie Chapman.

The investigation appeared to be going nowhere. Then, on September 30, 1888, the killer struck again, taking two victims in a single night. At around 1 a.m. on that Sunday morning, Louis Diemschutz was driving his pony cart towards Dutfield Yard, off Berner Street in Whitechapel. Diemschutz and his wife lived at the

International Working Men's Educational Club (IWMC) a club for Eastern European Jewish Socialists. He also served as caretaker.

As Diemschutz pulled into the club yard, he noticed an object lying on the ground near a wall. Striking a match, he saw that it was a woman. Diemschutz rushed into the club and got another member to help him. When they returned they noticed a stream of blood running from the woman's body. They then ran to find a policeman.

A few minutes later, Police Constable Henry Lamb and his associate arrived. Lamb felt for a pulse and detected none, although the body was still warm. Sending his associate to fetch a doctor, Lamb looked over the scene. There were no signs of a struggle and, unlike in the earlier cases, the woman's clothes hadn't been disturbed.

Dr. Frederick Blackwell arrived at 1:16 a.m. and carried out an examination of the body. There was a long cut to the neck, starting on the left, severing the blood vessels there, cutting right through the windpipe and terminating on the opposite side. The police surgeon, Dr. Phillips, had now arrived and the two doctors agreed that the time of death was sometime between 12:36 and 12:56 a.m. However, the chairman of the IWMC had walked through the yard at around 12:40 a.m. and seen nothing suspicious, narrowing the time of death even further. It appeared that Diemschutz might have disturbed the killer at his work.

Then, as the police searched the scene for clues, word came of another murder, just a quarter of a mile away, in Mitre Square.

A small quadrant of some 24 yards by 24, Mitre Square was surrounded mainly by commercial buildings and warehouses, with very few residences. At night, when the businesses were closed, the Square was a dark and secluded area.

At around 1:44 a.m. on September 30, Police Constable Edward Watkins was making his regular rounds through the area. He'd passed this way some fifteen minutes earlier. Then, he'd seen nothing untoward. Now, as he shone his lantern into a corner, he made a horrific discovery.

The body of a woman lay on the ground, positioned on her back with her feet facing in towards the square. Her clothes were pulled up above her waist. Her throat was cut and her stomach ripped open, her bowels protruding from the gaping wound. Her face, too, had suffered severe lacerations and there was blood pooled around her.

Watkins ran to one of the businesses in the square to fetch George Morris, a retired constable who worked as a night watchman. With his whistle, he summoned help from two more policemen and they conducted a search of the square to see if the killer might still be hiding there.

At 2:18, Dr. Frederick Gordon Brown arrived and carried out an examination of the victim. The woman's abdomen had been ripped open and she had terrible mutilations to her face. The body was still warm with no sign of rigor mortis setting in, leading Brown to conclude that she'd been dead less than half an hour.

The police, meanwhile, had fanned out in their hunt for the killer. At 2:55 a.m., Constable Alfred Long found a piece of a bloody apron lying in the entrance to a building on Goulston Street. Just above the apron, scrawled in white chalk on an archway were the words:

"The Juwes are

The men That

Will not

be Blamed

For nothing."

The piece of bloody apron was ascertained to come from the Mitre Square victim, which suggests that the chalk message might have been written by the killer. However, even as a constable was left to guard this potentially valuable clue, an instruction came from Sir Charles Warren, Commissioner of the Metropolitan Police, to obliterate the message. Warren would later explain his rationale for this highly controversial action by insisting that if the message had been seen by the public it might have sparked an onslaught against Jews, with resultant loss of life and destruction of property.

The police meanwhile had initiated their enquiries into these latest murders. The victim in Dutfield's Yard was soon identified as Elizabeth Stride, known locally as "Long Liz." Stride was a native of Sweden who had come to England as a domestic worker. She had been married to a man named John Stride, but after his death, she had lived with a laborer named Michael Kidney. Although she may have occasionally prostituted herself, her primary source of income was sewing or cleaning work. On the day of her death, she'd left her lodgings early in the evening without telling anyone where she was going. She had been killed by a deep cut to her throat, although there was no sign of strangulation (as there'd been in the Chapman murder).

A number of people had seen Stride just before her death. One of them was Constable William Smith, who saw her at around 12:30 talking to a man of about 30, with dark hair and a mustache.

Another witness, Israel Schwartz, said he saw a man trying to pull a woman into the street, then throw her down on the ground. Not wanting to get involved, Schwartz crossed to the opposite side of the road, where he spotted a second man standing, lighting his pipe. The man who threw the woman down called out to the other "Lipski!" Schwartz started to walk away but began running when one of the men started following him.

William Marshall who lived at 64 Berner Street, also reported seeing Stride on the night of the murder. He said she was talking to a middle-aged man, about 5-foot-six and somewhat stoutly built. Another eyewitness, James Brown reported a sighting of Liz at 12:45 a.m., just minutes before her death. He said he saw her talking to a man at the corner of Berner and Fairclough Streets. "Not tonight, some other night," he overheard her say. The man he described was about 5-foot-7 and wearing a long, dark overcoat.

Unfortunately, none of these descriptions got the police any closer to finding the suspect.

The woman murdered in Mitre Square was easily identified since she was carrying some pawn tickets in her pocket. Once publicized, a man named John Kelly came forward to identify her as Catharine Eddowes, his common-law wife.

Eddowes, known as Kate to her friends, had been a happy, easygoing woman. She was liked by all who knew her, although it was said that she could be difficult and quarrelsome when she'd been drinking. She had spent 20 years as the common-law wife of a man named Thomas Conway, a union that had produced three children. Conway's physical abuse and Kate's drinking had caused the relationship to break up in 1880. The next year, she met John Kelly. They'd remained together for the rest of her life. Kate's friends were adamant that she was not a prostitute, but there is evidence to suggest that she did occasionally prostitute herself, perhaps when under the influence of alcohol.

The evening before her death, Kate told John Kelly that she was going to visit her daughter to borrow some money. Kelly warned her about the Whitechapel killer but Kate scoffed at his warning. "Don't you fear for me," she said. "I'll take care of myself and I shan't fall into his hands."

Kate never made it to her daughter's house, but she did find money somewhere and ended up getting so drunk that she was locked up at Bishopsgate Street Police Station. At around 12:30 a.m., she woke from her drunken stupor and asked if she could go home.

"I shall get a damned fine hiding when I get home," she told Constable Hutt, the officer on duty.

"And serve you right," Hutt told her. "You have no right to get drunk."

Shortly after, Hutt allowed her to leave. It was around one o'clock in the morning.

Mitre Square was just a short, eight-minute walk away.

As with Polly Nichols and Annie Chapman, Kate Eddowes's throat had been deeply slashed from left to right. The resulting wound was the cause of death, but there were severe post-mortem mutilations, best described by Dr. Brown's testimony:

"The abdomen had been laid open from the breast bone to the pubes. The intestines had been detached to a large extent and about two feet of the colon was cut away. The peritoneal lining was cut through and the left kidney carefully taken out and removed. The left renal artery was cut through. I should say that someone who knew the position of the kidney must have done it. The womb was cut through horizontally, leaving a stump of ¾ of an inch. The rest of the womb had been taken away with some of the ligaments. The vagina and cervix of the womb were uninjured.

"The face was very much mutilated. There was a cut about ¼ of an inch through the lower left eyelid dividing the structures. The right eyelid was cut through to about ½ inch. There was a deep cut over the bridge of the nose extending from the left border of the nasal bone down near to the angle of the jaw of the right side. The tip of the nose was quite detached from the nose.

"Several other cuts were sustained on the face, plus the right ear lobe had been completely severed and had fallen from her clothing when she was taken to the morgue."

As police inquiries continued an important eyewitness emerged. Joseph Lawende said that he'd left the Imperial Club with two friends at around 1:35 a.m. The men saw a couple in conversation at Church Passage, near Mitre Square. Lawende described the man as young, medium height and with a small fair-colored mustache. He was wearing a dark jacket and a deerstalker's hat. Lawende wasn't able to see the woman's face, but accurately described Kate Eddowes' clothing. This sighting took place just 9 minutes before Eddowes was found dead.

But what of the enigmatic message scrawled on the wall, "The Juwes are the men that will not be blamed for nothing." It has never been firmly established that the message was left by the Whitechapel killer. Even if it was, it gets us no closer to uncovering his identity.

Another intriguing aspect of this case, one perhaps as infamous as the murders themselves, is the Ripper letters. Although hundreds of letters purporting to be from the killer were sent to the police, newspapers, and individuals associated with the case, only three have endured in the realm of Ripper lore. Two, in particular, which were written by the same individual, gave the killer his infamous epithet "Jack the Ripper," which had not existed up until then.

The first of these was received by the Central News Agency on September 27, 1888 and was addressed to "The Boss, Central News Office." Written in red ink, it read as follows:

25 Sept: 1888

Dear Boss

I keep on hearing the police have caught me but they wont fix me just yet. I have laughed when they look so clever and talk about being on the right track. That joke about Leather Apron gave me real fits. I am down on whores and I shant quit ripping them till I do get buckled. Grand work the last job was. I gave the lady no time to squeal. How can they catch me now. I love my work and want to start again. You will soon hear of me with my funny little games. I saved some proper red stuff in a ginger beer bottle over the last job to write with but it went thick like glue and I cant use it. Red ink is fit enough I hope ha.ha. The next job I do I shall clip. The lady's ears off and send to the Police officers just for jolly wouldn't you. Keep this letter back till I do a bit more work then give it out straight. My knife's so nice and sharp I want to get to work right away if I get a chance.

Good luck.

Yours truly

Jack the Ripper

Don't mind me giving the trade name

The editor considered the letter as a hoax and debated whether he should send it to the police for a couple of days. The night that the police eventually received it, Liz Stride and Kate Eddowes were murdered.

On the Monday morning following the murders, the Central News Agency received another letter in the same handwriting as the one received on September 25. It was postmarked October 1:

"I wasn't codding dear old Boss when I gave you the tip. youll hear about saucy Jackys work tomorrow double event this time number one squealed a bit couldn't finish straight off. had not time to get ears for police thanks for keeping last letter back till I got to work again.

Jack the Ripper"

Unlike the news editor, the police believed these letters to be a genuine clue.   Facsimiles were placed outside every police station in the hope that someone might recognize the handwriting. However, all this generated was a new deluge of crank letters.

The third letter was sent on October 16 to George Lusk, head of the Mile End Vigilance Committee. Accompanying this letter was a section of kidney, which the writer claimed was taken from one of the victims. The Vigilance Committee members were not convinced, so they took the kidney to Dr. Thomas Openshaw at the London Hospital to examine. Dr. Openshaw confirmed that it was indeed a human adult kidney, which had been preserved in spirits rather than in formalin, as would be used in hospitals.

The letter that accompanied the kidney was not written by the author of the two earlier letters signed Jack the Ripper.

"From hell

Mr Lusk

Sor

I send you half the Kidne I took from one women prasarved it for you the other piece I fried and ate it was very nise I may send you the bloody knif that took it out if you only wate a whil longer

Signed

Catch me when

You can

Mishter Lusk"

Whether any of these letters were from the real Jack the Ripper is a matter of passionate debate among Ripperologists. Ripper expert Philip Sugden believes that the two letters signed Jack the Ripper are fakes. Others point to information presented in this letter that only the killer could have known, specifically the severing of Kate Eddowes earlobe and the forecast of the "double event." However, on closer scrutiny, these are easily explained away.

First, the claim that he will send the police the victim's ears. This never happened. While it is true that Kate Eddowes' one ear lobe was cut off, the killer had plenty of time to carry through with his promise to snip off both earlobes and send them to the police. He never did so.

Then there's the "forecast" of the "double event." In fact, by the time the letter was sent on either September 31 or October 1, the East End was already abuzz with news of the double murder.

Sir Charles Warren, who headed up the Metropolitan Police during the Ripper's murderous spree, also regarded the first two letters as a hoax. Modern day criminal profilers like the FBI's John Douglas share this view. "It's too organized, too indicative of intelligence and rationale thought, and far too 'cutesy,' Douglas says. "An offender of this type would never think of his actions as 'funny little games' or say that his 'knife's so nice and sharp.'"

The letter sent to Lusk is a far better candidate for the real thing. The kidney was certainly human and was found to be from a person suffering Bright's Disease. Kate Eddowes did indeed suffer from this affliction, but that neither proves that the kidney was hers or that the letter came from the real Jack the Ripper. As with so much about this case, we will probably never know the truth.

In the wake of the "Double Event," Whitechapel went into lockdown. The once boisterous streets were virtually deserted after dark with many of the prostitutes finding lodging with friends or family. Trade also suffered. Many Londoners were afraid even to set foot in Whitechapel, for fear of falling into the hands of a monster whose legend had by now assumed near mythic proportions.

Both uniformed and plainclothes policemen flooded into the area walking the streets during the hours of darkness, while the Mile

End Vigilance Committee hired men to patrol, equipped with billy clubs and police whistles.

Meanwhile, police officers systematically worked their way through the area's many lodging houses, questioning over 2,000 lodgers. They also distributed some 80,000 handbills throughout the neighborhood:

"POLICE NOTICE

TO THE OCCUPIER

On the morning of Friday, 31st August, Saturday 8th, and Sunday, 30th September, 1888, Women were murdered in or near Whitechapel, supposed by some one residing in the immediate neighborhood. Should you know of any person to whom suspicion is attached, you are earnestly requested to communicate at once with the nearest Police Station, Metropolitan Police Office, 30th September, 1888."

Special attention was paid to individuals working in certain occupations. Some 76 butchers and slaughterers were interrogated, plus many sailors working on the Thames River boats. A team of bloodhounds was trained and deployed in the area, with the hope that they might lead police to the killer. Meanwhile, a number of male officers were disguised as prostitutes and deployed to various street corners in the hope of luring the Ripper.

None of these methods helped in capturing the elusive Jack, but they did have the effect of calming tensions in Whitechapel. A month passed without another murder, the streets gradually got back to normal, prostitutes returned to ply their trade. But if the people of Whitechapel believed that the Ripper had moved on, they were about to be proved wrong – in the most brutal of fashions.

Mary Kelly was a pretty, young Irish prostitute, who'd arrived in London from Limerick, via Wales. She rented a first floor room at Miller's Court in Dorset Street, but at the beginning of November 1888, she was beset by money problems and several weeks behind with the rent. Her lover, Joe Barnett, was of no help either, unemployed and flat broke. Kelly and Barnett had recently had an argument and he'd moved out of their shared room. But the spat was short-lived. On Thursday night, November 8, the couple got together, and Barnett apologized for his behavior and for not having any money to give her.

People who knew Mary, described her as tall and pretty, with a pleasant demeanor. Others noted that she could be abusive when drunk, but in general, she was well liked and well thought of.

On the morning of Friday, November 9, 1888, Mary's landlord, John McCarthy, sent his assistant, Thomas Bowyer, to see if Mary was home and if she had any money for the rent. Bowyer arrived at 13 Miller's Court and knocked at the door. Getting no reply, he walked to the window and, reaching through a broken pane, pulled the curtain aside. What Bowyer saw sent him running back to his employer. McCarthy then went to see for himself before rushing off to find a constable.

The constable was talking with police officer Walter Dew when McCarthy approached. They went immediately to 13 Miller's Court and after peaking through the window and verifying what McCarthy had told them, Dew sent for Inspector Abberline.

Abberline and police surgeon, Dr. George Bagster Phillips, were soon on the scene. They opened the door to the small, cluttered room, where Mary's body lay on the bed, so severely mutilated that it was barely recognizable as human. These mutilations are best described by the medical examiner's report, filed by veteran pathologist Dr. Thomas Bond, who was brought into the case specifically to determine the extent of the killer's medical knowledge.

"The body was lying naked in the middle of the bed, the shoulders flat, but the axis of the body inclined to the left side of the bed...The whole of the surface of the abdomen and thighs was removed and the abdominal cavity emptied of its viscera. The breasts were cut off, the arms mutilated by several jagged wounds and the face hacked beyond recognition of the features and the tissues of the neck were severed all round down to the bone. The viscera were found in various parts: the uterus and kidney with one breast under the head, the other breast by the right foot, the liver between the feet, the intestines by the right side and the spleen by the left side. The flaps removed from the abdomen and thighs were on a table.

"Her face was gashed in all directions, the nose, cheeks, eyebrows & ears being partly removed. The lips were blanched and cut by several incisions running obliquely down to the chin. There were also numerous cuts extending irregularly across all of the features.

"The skin and tissues of the abdomen from the costal arch to the pubes were removed in three large flaps. The right thigh was denuded in front to the bone, the flap of skin including the external organs of generation and part of the right buttock. The left thigh was stripped of skin, fascia & muscles as far as the knee."

Dr. Bond's report continued for several more paragraphs, cataloging in minute detail the ferocious destruction of Mary Kelly's body. As he and Dr. Phillips tried to account for all of the organs, they realized that the killer had removed the heart and carried it away with him.

Cause of death was given as severance of the carotid artery with all of the mutilations carried out postmortem. As to the time of death, Dr. Bond judged this to have occurred between one and two o'clock in the morning. He stressed, however, that this was approximate given the time that had elapsed between the murder and the discovery of the body.

There seemed little doubt that the man who had killed Mary Kelly was the same monster who was responsible for the other four recently committed murders. All of the women had been killed with a very sharp knife of at least six inches in length and an inch in width. Dr. Bond sprung a surprise, though, when asked about the medical skill of the Ripper. He said that the killer possessed no anatomical knowledge at all, not even that of a butcher or slaughterer. This position is starkly different to that of other physicians who examined the bodies. Many Ripper experts believe that Dr. Bond's opinion was influenced by his belief that no medical professional could have committed such atrocities.

A new wave of panic swept through Whitehall as the streets were once again abandoned to the police patrols. There were sporadic incidents of mob violence, directed at anyone thought to be acting suspiciously. The police came under renewed pressure to catch the killer, and even Queen Victoria weighed in with criticism of their efforts.

Yet there was no lack of application on the part of the Police Force. They followed up every lead, chased down and interrogated every suspect. All of it came to nothing. The murderer had left behind not a clue, and while there were a number of eyewitnesses, a disagreement between the physicians, as to time of death, complicated things. Dr. Bond said Kelly had died between 1 a.m. and 2 a.m. Dr. Phillips felt it was later, between 4 and 5.

One of the witnesses, George Hutchinson, seemed to verify the later time. Hutchinson was a laborer who knew Mary Kelly. He said that he met Mary at about 2 a.m. on Friday morning. She asked him for some money and when he said he had none she walked away, but soon stopped to talk to another man.

According to Hutchinson, the man placed his arm around Mary's shoulders and they set off together, walking towards Dorset Street. He followed at a distance and saw them stop and talk for about three minutes. The man said something to Mary and she replied, "Alright my dear come along you will be comfortable." The man then placed his arm on Mary's shoulder and kissed her. They walked from there to Mary's room and entered. Hutchinson waited outside for about 40 minutes to see if they'd come out again. When they didn't, he left.

Asked to describe the man, Hutchinson said that he was mid-thirties, about 5-foot-6, with dark eyes, dark hair, and a small mustache. He was wearing a long dark coat, light waistcoat, dark trousers, and a dark felt hat turned down in the middle. He was very respectable looking with a "Jewish appearance."

Several other people reported seeing Mary on the night she died. Mary Ann Cox, another prostitute, saw Mary going into Miller's Court with a man at 11:45 p.m. Mary was very drunk. The man was described as about 36 years old, 5-foot-6, with a pale complexion and blotches on his face. He had small side-whiskers and a thick "carroty" mustache. He was dressed in shabby, dark clothes, dark overcoat, and black felt hat.

Laundress Sarah Lewis said that on the Wednesday before the murder, she'd been approached by a man of about forty years of age, who was fairly short, pale-faced, with a black mustache. The man wore a short black coat and carried a black bag about one foot long. He asked her to go with him but she refused. At around 2:30 a.m. on the night Mary Kelly was murdered, Sarah saw the same man in Miller's Court but managed to elude him. Just before 4 a.m. on that same morning, Lewis heard a woman shriek, "Murder!" Another woman also heard the cry.

Although there are similarities to the eyewitness reports, Inspector Abberline seemed to pay most credence to the account given by Hutchinson and even had Hutchinson walking around Whitechapel in the company of two police officers, to see if he could spot Mary's client again. Yet the question remains, why had Hutchinson followed Mary and her client in the first place? No viable explanation has ever been given and one has to wonder whether the story was concocted by Hutchinson, either to insert himself into the investigation or to deflect suspicion from himself. We shall never know.

With the murder of Mary Kelly, Jack the Ripper's campaign of terror in the East End of London appears to have run its course. As the months passed and the police exhausted what meager leads they had, the investigation wound down. It appeared the Ripper was gone for good.

However, there are two more murders that bear mentioning, simply because some writers have suggested that Jack may have been responsible. The first was Alice McKenzie, found with her throat slashed in July of 1889, the second Frances Coles, killed by a similar method in February 1891. Neither of the victims was mutilated, and the cuts to their throats were different to the other Ripper victims. Make of that what you will.

Suspects

No examination of the Whitechapel murders would be complete without an exploration of the main suspects, both those considered at the time of the murders and subsequently. These range from the ludicrous (Prince Albert Victor, Walter Sickert) to the improbable (Francis Tumblety, George Chapman).

It is this writer's believe that the Ripper was someone other than the suspects who are commonly mentioned. Nonetheless, let's examine what we know about Jack, and see how the leading candidates stack up.

Based on various eyewitness reports, we are able to build up a partial description of the killer. The Ripper was said to be:

- A white male

- Average or below average height

- Strongly built

- Between 20 and 40 years of age.

- Respectably dressed

To that, we are able to add the opinion of the pathologists who examined the victims that Jack:

- Was right-handed

- Had some medical expertise (although there are contrary opinions)

We can also safely assume that he:

- Lived in the East End, as he must have known the area well in order to so easily evade the police

- Had a regular job since the murders all occurred on weekends

- Was single so that he could roam the streets at all hours

The three main suspects at the time of the Ripper murders, and in their immediate aftermath, were:

Montague John Druitt: a doctor who disappeared at around the time of Mary Kelly's murder and whose body was pulled from the Thames on December 31, 1888. Druitt was known to have fought a lifelong battle with depression. His death was ruled a suicide.

Although Druitt was the right age and height, he was slightly built, quite unlike the stocky man described at the crime scenes. He also lived some distance away, in Blackheath, and was not known to frequent the East End. In addition, he had an alibi for at least one of the murders (Annie Chapman).

Nonetheless, the timing of Druitt's death, coinciding as it did with the last of the Whitechapel murders, marked him out as a suspect. Police Commissioner Sir Charles Warren, was known to consider him the most viable suspect. However, the most knowledgeable man on the Whitechapel murders, Chief Inspector Abberline, did not believe Druitt was the Ripper.

Aaron Kosminski: a Polish Jew who lived in Whitechapel and was said to hate women in general and prostitutes in particular. The main piece of evidence against Kosminski is that he was removed to a lunatic asylum shortly after the last Ripper murder (he supposedly died soon after). This is put forward as a reason why the murders stopped when they did.

However, the facts do not support the theory in this case. Kosminski was not removed to an asylum in March 1889, as stated, but sometime in 1891. And he did not die soon afterwards, he remained incarcerated for another 25 years during which time he was described as a "harmless imbecile."

Are we to believe that the Ripper, having committed five extraordinary murders in just three months, would then suddenly lay dormant for two whole years before his incarceration? Highly unlikely. And Kosminski, short and slight of frame, did not match eyewitness descriptions either, neither did he possess any medical skill.

Michael Ostrog: a confidence man who passed himself off as a doctor and, who was later detained in a lunatic asylum. Ostrog is perhaps the least likely candidate of the original suspects. At 60, he was way too old and, at 5-foot-11, he was much too tall. He was also never known to be violent and, despite passing himself off as a surgeon, he possessed no medical knowledge. Ostrog seems to be considered simply because he lied about his whereabouts during the three months of the Ripper murders. Then again, as a con man, lies were his stock in trade and he could have been lying to conceal any number of criminal activities.

So if Druitt, Kosminski, and Ostrog are disregarded, who else is there? A number of other possible Rippers have also been proposed in the years since the crimes were committed, including:

Prince Albert Victor: Grandson of Queen Victoria and second in line to the British throne. This ludicrous theory hinges on the Prince fathering a child by an East End prostitute and then concocting a plot to get rid of the child's mother and all of her prostitute friends who knew of his indiscretion. Various sub-theories have Sir William Gull, the royal physician, as the Ripper, acting under orders from Queen Victoria herself.

Even if we take this theory seriously, it is a matter of record that Prince Albert was in Scotland when some of the murders were committed. As for Gull, he was 70 years old in 1888 and had recently suffered a stroke.

Walter Sickert: Almost as ridiculous is the notion, proffered by best-selling author, Patricia Cornwell, that renowned English painter, Walter Sickert was the Ripper. Cornwell's theory is based primarily on the belief that some of Sickert's paintings (completed 20 years after the event) resemble the Ripper crime scenes. This hypothesis has met with widespread ridicule, from Ripper experts and crime historians alike.

James Maybrick: A theory that surfaced in 1992, when a Liverpool scrap metal dealer, Michael Barrett, claimed to have found the diary of a cotton broker named James Maybrick, who died in 1889. In this diary, Maybrick confesses to being Jack the Ripper.

Despite the initial excitement this caused among Ripperologists, the diary was subsequently found to be a forgery, and Barrett eventually admitted to the hoax.

Francis Tumbelty: Another candidate who has been put forward in recent times is Francis Tumbelty, an American quack doctor who was a known sadist and who was in London at the time of the Ripper murders.

There are a number of reasons why Tumbelty could not have been Jack. For starters, he was 55 years old in 1888, much older than the man seen by eyewitnesses. Secondly, despite making a fortune from quack medicines, he had no medical training. There's also nothing to suggest that he was ever violent towards women. In fact, Tumbelty was a homosexual, and as we now know, homosexual serial killers tend to prey on men, not women.

Which brings us to the favored suspect of Chief Inspector Abberline.

On the face of it, **George Chapman** (real name: Severin Antoniovich Klosowski) ticks many of the boxes. He was apprenticed to a surgeon while living in his native Poland; he'd moved to London 18 months before the murders started and was living in Whitechapel for their duration; he was known to be violent towards women and would eventually be hanged for poisoning three of his wives; he was single at that time and had the freedom to roam the streets at all hours; he worked a regular job which meant he was occupied during the week but free on weekends.

However, there are also many reasons to question his candidacy. One is age; Chapman was 23 years old in 1888, younger than the man seen by witnesses. Eyewitnesses accounts are often unreliable, though, and Chapman may simply have looked older than his years. But even if we overlook age, we encounter another problem when we consider why a man who'd savagely murdered 5 women within 3 months would suddenly stop. Chapman remained in London for two more years before immigrating to America in 1891 (he'd return to England just a year later). So if he was Jack the Ripper, why did he suddenly stop killing?

But perhaps the most significant reason for questioning George Chapman's inclusion as a Ripper suspect is the difference between the Ripper murders and the crimes for which he was eventually hanged, the poisoning deaths of three women. Is it possible to reconcile the homicidal maniac, Jack the Ripper, with the coolly, calculating poisoner, George Chapman? Inspector Abberline seemed to think so, but he was working without the wealth of knowledge we now have about serial killers. Suffice to say that if George Chapman and Jack the Ripper were one and the same person, the change in modus operandi would be without precedent.

And so, despite the millions of research hours and the copious works produced on the subject, the identity of the world's most infamous serial killer remains a mystery. We shall probably never know who Jack the Ripper was. Perhaps, that is as it should be.

The Axeman Of New Orleans

It was May 22, 1918, and with war raging in Europe, Andrew Maggio, a barber in the city of New Orleans, had just received his call-up papers. Distressed at the prospect of being drafted, Andrew took to the city's taverns for a night of drinking. He returned to the room he shared with his brother, Jake, at around 2 am, somewhat the worse for wear.

Andrew and Jake's rooms abutted the home of their married brother, Joseph. At around 4.a.m. on the morning of May 23, Jake woke to the sound of groaning. Realizing that the sounds were coming from next door, he banged on the wall, trying to rouse his brother. When this failed to elicit a response, he tried again. Still nothing.

Fearful now, he stepped over to Andrew's bed and after some effort was able to wake him. Together, they crept along the passage to Joseph's apartment. To their alarm, they found evidence of a break-in. A wooden panel had been removed from the kitchen door. It lay on the ground, with a chisel on top of it.

Entering the home via the kitchen, the brothers made their way to Joseph's bedroom. He lay on the bed, legs draped over the side, his wife, Catherine, lying partially over him. Running to his side, Jake and Andrew checked for signs of life and found their brother to be barely alive, with deep gashes on his head and blood everywhere. Catherine was already dead. They immediately called the police and an ambulance was dispatched. It was too late. By the time help arrived, Joseph Maggio was dead.

The first officer to arrive was Corporal Arthur Hatener and he went immediately inside to look for clues. He found a scene of unprecedented carnage. Joseph Maggio and his wife lay across the bloodstained bed. From the evidence, it appeared that the killer had gained entry through the kitchen door then proceeded to the bedroom. There, he'd struck Mrs. Maggio in the head before slitting her throat with a razor, nearly decapitating her. He'd then used the axe on Joseph (presumably as he rose) before slashing him with the razor too.

A search of the premises soon turned up the murder weapons, the axe lying in the bathroom where the murderer had made some effort to clean it, the razor lying close to the bodies.

With a crowd gathering outside, the coroner arrived and set the time of death at between two and three in the morning. Then, as the victims were removed, a woman came forward and told investigators that she had seen Andrew lurking outside the house during the early morning hours. Jake and Andrew were taken in for questioning and despite their protestations of innocence, they were locked up.

The following day, Jake was released while Andrew remained in prison. The police had learned, in the meanwhile, that the razor used to cut the throats of Joseph and Catherine Maggio belonged to Andrew. In fact, one of his employees had seen him remove it from his barbershop on the day prior to the murders. Andrew admitted that he had done so, but insisted that it was to repair a nick in the blade. Nonetheless, it looked bad for him.

Visibly nervous, Andrew now concocted a new story, claiming he'd seen a man lurking outside the house when he'd returned from the bar. It seemed a fortuitous recollection and the police weren't buying it. They believed that the killer had been familiar with the layout of the house. That made Andrew a strong suspect.

Still, there were other bits of evidence that pointed away from him. A number of witnesses confirmed that he'd been heavily intoxicated that night and, according to Jake, he'd been sound asleep when the murders occurred. Without sufficient evidence to charge him, the police were forced to let Andrew Maggio go. They soon had another line of inquiry to follow.

About a block from the Maggio's house the police discovered a strange message, scrawled in chalk on the sidewalk. It read: "Mrs. Maggio will sit up tonight just like Mrs. Toney." It seemed like an important clue, yet initial inquiries turned up nothing. Then, someone recalled another series of crimes, startlingly similar to the Maggio double-homicide, which had occurred seven years earlier, in 1911.

The three horrendous axe murders that had occurred back then remained unsolved. Like the Maggios, the victims were Italians grocers who had been asleep in their beds at the time of the attacks. In each of the cases, the murderer had gained access by removing a panel in the back door.

The third of those attacks had been against a Mr. Tony Schiambra and his wife. The police now believed that the "Mrs. Toney" mentioned in the chalk message, was a reference to Mrs. Schiambra.

At the time of these murders, the talk within the New Orleans Italian community had been about a possible Mafia connection in the crimes. The victims had all been Italian business people. Perhaps, they'd failed to pay "protection money" or had taken loans they couldn't repay. But the power of the mob had been broken in New Orleans, or at least so people believed. Perhaps the murder of the Maggios proved this wasn't so.

While the police were still contemplating these possibilities another murder occurred, one that seemed to discount their Mafia theory. About two weeks after the Maggio attack, on June 6, a baker named John Zanca made a delivery of bread to one of his regular customers, a grocery named Louis Besumer. On arrival, he found Besumer's store still locked, which was unusual. The 59-year-old Polish shopkeeper was always up early, waiting for his bread.

Zanca went around to knock at the side door and had just done so when he heard movement from inside. In the next moment, the door opened and   Besumer staggered through, his face was covered in blood. He said that someone had attacked him and his wife and pointed to the bedroom. Moving with trepidation, Zanca entered the room where he found a woman sprawled across the blood-soaked bed.

Zanca wanted to call the police immediately, but Besumer inexplicably tried to stop him, insisting that he should call a private physician. However, Zanca ignored the request and summoned both the police and an ambulance.

The police arrived to a familiar scene, a panel removed from the back door and the weapon, a bloody hatchet, left behind by the assailant. As the female victim (who turned out not to be Mrs. Besumer, but a Miss Anna Harriett Lowe) was taken to hospital, the police questioned Besumer, but he was unable to give a description of either the attack or the attacker.

Suspicion initially fell on one of Besumer's employees, but he was released after questioning. Then Anna Lowe briefly regained consciousness and told the police a number of conflicting stories. First, she said that she'd been attacked by a "mulatto." Then she told a different version of events, claiming it was Besumer who had struck her with the axe. Anna died soon afterwards, but not before adding to her initial accusations. She now claimed that Besumer was a German spy involved in a conspiracy against the United States. The papers soon picked up this story and ran with it, concocting a fanciful tale involving trunk loads of secret documents, stashes of opiates and coded messages written in German, Russian, and Yiddish.

The police, though, weren't convinced by the spy story. Neither were they sure that Besumer had had anything to do with Anna's murder. That is, until Besumer asked to be involved in the investigation of the crime. This strange request immediately aroused suspicion and the police became convinced that Besumer had something to hide. They began to think that the attack was the result of a domestic quarrel and that the story of an intruder had been concocted by Besumer to cover his tracks. In short order, Besumer found himself under arrest for murder.

Yet it was quite clear that Besumer was not New Orleans Axeman. Two months after the attack on Anna Lowe, that fiend struck again. On August 5, a businessman named Edward Schneider arrived home after working late at the office. He expected his pregnant wife to meet him at the door, but the house was silent. He called to his wife but got no response.

Walking from room to room with growing apprehension, he came into the bedroom, where he saw his wife lying on the bed, covered in blood. Edward rushed to her side and noticed that she had a gaping head wound and that some of her teeth were knocked out. But she was still breathing. Wasting no time, he summoned first an ambulance and then the police.

Mrs. Schneider spent several days in the hospital in critical condition but eventually recovering consciousness. However, she could recall hardly anything about the attack. She said that she had been taking a nap when something had awoken her and she'd seen a dark figure looming over her. Then the axe came down and knocked her out cold.

Fortunately, the attack had no effect on her pregnancy. She stayed in the hospital, and a week later delivered a healthy daughter.

The newspapers meanwhile had picked up on the series of attacks. In August, they ran a story under the banner 'IS AN AXEMAN AT LARGE IN NEW ORLEANS?' Needless to say, this caused panic. As the terrified populace cowered in their homes and armed themselves, stories abounded of mysterious axe-wielding strangers, lurking in the shadows.

Early on the morning of August 10, five days after the Schneider attack, Pauline and Mary Bruno were awakened by loud thumps coming from their Uncle Joseph's room. Pauline sat up in bed and saw a tall, dark figure in her room. She screamed, causing the man to turn and flee. The girl would later say that he moved as though he had wings.

In the next moment, her uncle, Joseph Romano, appeared in the doorway. His nightshirt was drenched in blood from there were gashes on his face. "Call the hospital," he gasped before collapsing to the floor. He died of his wounds two days later.

A new wave of panic swept the city, fuelled by penchant of New Orleanians for story telling. The Axeman was suddenly spotted everywhere and reports of mysterious strangers flooded police precincts. One man told of waking up in the middle of the night to scraping sounds at his door. Panicked, he fired off a couple of rounds. The following day the police were called and found clear signs of someone trying to gain entry via a door panel.

A popular theory of the time was that the Axeman was able to move around undetected by disguising himself as a woman. Retired detective, Joseph Dantonio, offered another explanation. He believed the Axeman to be a Jekyll and Hyde type character, able to blend in with the citizenry until the homicidal urge took him and he was forced to kill again.

But just as the Axeman panic was at its peak, the killer dropped out of sight. As the months passed, New Orleans eventually settled back into its normal routines. People wondered if he had left the area or been killed, or if his bloodlust had been sated. The war ended and life began to take on the veneer of normality. Then, just when everyone had begun to believe that the killer was gone for good, he struck again.

On Monday, March 10, 1919, Iorlando Jordano heard a series of bloodcurdling screams coming from next door. He ran to help and walked in on a terrible scene. His neighbor, Rosie Cortimiglia, was sitting on the floor, gravely injured, her dead two-year-old daughter cradled in her arms. Her husband Charles, a grocer, lay nearby in a pool of blood.

The police were called and arrived soon after. Rosie said that the attack had happened while the family slept. Her baby had been asleep in her arms and had been killed by a single blow to the back of the head. Her husband had grappled with the attacker but had been overcome.

As the police combed the house and immediate area, they found the Axeman's familiar signature, a panel chiseled out of the kitchen door, a bloodstained axe left at the scene. It looked as though the homicidal maniac was back.

But, once Rosie Cortimiglia recovered from her injuries, she had a different tale to tell. She said that Iorlando Jordano, the man who had come to her assistance was the attacker, along with his father, Frank. The motive, she said, was business rivalry. The Jordanos were promptly arrested. They would later be found guilty, and based solely on Rosie's testimony, Iorlando got the death sentence, while his father was sentenced to life in prison.

About three days after the Cortimiglia attack, the editor of the Times-Picayune newspaper received a letter that purportedly came from the killer. Dated, "Hell, March 13, 1919," it echoed the infamous letters attributed to the Whitechapel murderer, Jack the Ripper. The writer taunted the police for their failure to solve the crimes and promised more violence to come. He even gave a date for the next murder (the following Tuesday, March 19) and stated that he would not call on any home where a jazz band was playing.

The letter was almost certainly a hoax, but the citizens of New Orleans took it very seriously. It is said that there's never been a more raucous evening in The Big Easy than St. Joseph's Night, March 19, 1919. Jazz music blared out from every homestead, every apartment. And no one was murdered that night.

In April, Louis Besumer went on trial and was acquitted of the murder of his mistress, Anna Harriett Lowe. With the war now over, the accusations of espionage were also given short shrift and Besumer walked away a free man.

Four months later, on August 10, the Axeman struck again, attacking Steve Boca, another Italian grocer, while he slept. Boca was struck with an axe but managed to stumble out of his house and summon help. His assailant had gained entry by chiseling a panel from the door and the axe was left in the kitchen.

Then, on September 3, someone broke into home of Sarah Laumann. The 19-year-old girl was found unconscious in her bed, with multiple wounds to her head. A bloody axe was left outside in the yard. Laumann survived, the next victim would not.

In the early hours of October 27, Mike Pepitone was attacked while he slept. Hearing a struggle from his bedroom, his wife went to investigate, almost   colliding with a man fleeing the scene. Their daughter ran for the police, summoning Deputy Ben Corcoran. Upon his arrival, the officer found Mrs. Pepitone standing over her husband. "It looks like the Axeman was here and murdered Mike," she said. Pepitone was transported to Charity Hospital, where he later died.

Upon investigation, the police found a panel chiseled from a door and a bloody axe lying on the porch. Yet, there were aspects of the case that didn't add up. Mrs. Pepitone claimed that she had seen two men in her home, not just one. Yet, she hadn't screamed on encountering them. She also did not appear in any way distraught as she answered police questions. Police suspicions aside, there was nothing to connect Mrs. Pepitone to the crime. Mike Pepitone went down as the last victim of the mysterious New Orleans Axeman.

The murders were never solved, the killer never apprehended. But in 1920, two events occurred that help to throw some light on the case. On December 7, 1920, Rosie Cortimiglia retracted her accusation against the Jordanos, admitting that she'd lied about them killing her husband. The assailant, she said, had been a man who was not known to her. Both Iorlando and Frank Jordano were released.

The other event had occurred five days earlier, on the other side of the country, in Los Angeles, California. On that day, Mrs. Mike Pepitone, dressed all in black, stepped from a doorway to gun down a New Orleans native named Joseph Mumfre. Mumfre was killed instantly and, as he lay on the sidewalk, Mrs. Pepitone waited patiently for the police to come and arrest her. She insisted that Mumfre was the man she'd seen running from her husband's room on the night he was murdered. She would eventually serve three years of a ten-year sentence before being released.

As the police looked into Mumfre's background they found that he did have a criminal record and that his prison history bore an eerie correlation with the Axeman murders. During the break in the killings, from 1911 and 1918, Mumfre was in prison. He was also incarcerated between the last murder in 1918 and the first murder in 1919. During the time of each of the murders, he was free and he left New Orleans directly after Pepitone was killed.

So, was Joseph Mumfre the New Orleans Axeman? Aside from Mrs. Pepitone's testimony, there is no evidence that directly links him to any of the crimes, but there were no more axe murders in New Orleans after his death.

The Boston Strangler

It is one of the most infamous serial killer cases in U.S history, the first case extensively covered by mass-market television, radio and the national press, a case that sparked widespread panic in the city of Boston, a case that continues to fascinate, even to this day.

Between June 1962 and January 1964, 13 Massachusetts women fell victim to a serial killer, a fiend who has gone down in history by the notorious epithet, the Boston Strangler. The killer entered the homes of his victims without force, apparently talking his way in. Once inside, he sexually molested the women before strangling them with articles of clothing and fleeing the scene. Many of the victims were posed, others had sexually degrading post-mortem acts performed upon them, all were killed in their own homes.

Albert De Salvo, a hyper-sexed factory worker, sex offender and petty criminal, confessed to the crimes, and although he was never officially charged with the murders, he entered the public consciousness as the Strangler, a belief that held for decades. Yet there is significant evidence to suggest that De Salvo was not the killer. Indeed, many of the detectives working the case believed that the murders were not the work of a single man but of two, and possibly more, perpetrators, working independently.

The first murder occurred on June 14, 1962. Anna Slesers, a 55-year-old divorcee living in the Back Bay area was due to attend a memorial service that evening and had arranged for her son, Juris, to pick her up at 7 o'clock. However, when Juris arrived at his mother's apartment, there was no reply.

At first, Juris was annoyed, then concerned, when his pounding on the door brought no response. Eventually, he applied his shoulder to the door and forced it open. His worst fears were confirmed as he walked through the apartment and saw his mother lying on the bathroom floor with the cord from her robe wound tightly around her neck.

Responding to the call, detectives James Mellon and John Driscoll found the petite woman provocatively displayed, the cloth cord of her housecoat knotted around her neck, and tied in a decorative bow. The apartment appeared to have been ransacked, although a gold watch and several pieces of jewelry, left out in the open, had not been taken.

Just a couple of weeks later, on June 30, there was another murder. Nina Nichols lived alone in an apartment in the Brighton area of Boston. The 68-year-old, retired physiotherapist was found sexually assaulted and strangled with a pair of nylon stockings, the ends knotted in a bow. As with the Slesers murder, Nina Nichols' body had been posed and the apartment ransacked, although none of her valuables had been taken.

That same day, in the suburb of Lynn, some 15 miles north of Boston, an almost identical murder was committed. Helen Blake, a 65-year-old divorcee, was raped, and then strangled with a stocking, her body left suggestively posed. Her apartment had been thoroughly ransacked, but although two diamond rings were missing, other valuables were left untouched.

This latest murder set alarm bells jangling at police headquarters. Three homicides in a relatively small area, over a period of just two weeks, all of them bearing a clear signature, and quite possibly committed by the same man. As Police Commissioner Edmund McNamara canceled all police leave and put detectives on the ground checking on known sex offenders, a warning went out via the media to Boston's women. They were advised to keep doors locked and to be wary of admitting strangers to their homes.

These measures didn't deter the Strangler at all. On August 21, 75-year-old, Ida Irga, was found dead in her apartment. The shy, retiring widow had been strangled with a pillowcase, her nude body posed flat on its back, each ankle resting on a chair, the placement (facing the door) designed for maximum shock value. She'd been dead two days by the time she was found.

Just 24 hours later, came another grisly discovery. Jane Sullivan, a 67-year-old nurse, lived across town from Ida Irga, in Dorchester. She had been dead for 10 days before her body was found, laid out in her bathtub. The condition of the corpse made it impossible to determine whether she'd been sexually assaulted or not.

As panic gripped the city of Boston, there was a three-month reprieve before the next murder. This crime, however, was somewhat different. Up until now, the Strangler had targeted older victims, but Sophie Clark, an attractive, African-American student, was just 21-years-old. On December 5, 1962, Sophie's roommates returned home to find her nude body, lying legs apart, three nylon stockings knotted tightly around her neck. She'd been sexually assaulted and there was semen found on the rug close to her body.

There was no sign of forced entry which Sophie's roommates thought was strange. They assured the detectives that Sophie had been extremely security conscious, insisting on an extra lock on the door and even questioning friends before admitting them to the apartment.

As police questioned the neighbors, an interesting lead turned up. Mrs. Marcella Lulka told officers that around 2:20 that afternoon a man had knocked on her door and said that the building manager had sent him to speak to her about painting her apartment. He'd then complimented her on her figure, and asked if she'd ever thought of modeling.

Mrs. Lulka had asked the man to be quiet, by raising a finger to her lips. She'd told him that her husband was asleep in the next room and he'd then said it was the wrong apartment and hurried away. The man was 25 to 30 years old, she said, of average height with honey-colored hair. He'd been wearing a dark jacket and dark green trousers.

A check with the building manager revealed that he hadn't engaged anyone to do any painting, leading police to suspect that this man was the Strangler, especially as Sophie Clark was killed at around 2:30 in the afternoon. Why, though, had the security conscious Sophie let him in?

Three weeks after the murder of Sophie Clark, a 23-year-old secretary named Patricia Bissette failed to show up for work. Her boss was concerned about her, so he called on her apartment. Getting no response when he knocked, he tracked down the building superintendent and the two of them entered the apartment through a window.

They found Patricia Bissette lying face up in bed, the covers drawn up to her chin. Several stockings were knotted around her neck.

The medical examiner would later confirm that she'd been raped and possibly sodomized.

On Wednesday, May 8, 1963, friends of Beverly Samans, a 23-year-old graduate student, became concerned when she didn't show up for choir practice at the Second Unitarian Church in Back Bay. A friend went to her apartment to check on Beverley, entering with a key that she had given him. As the man opened the front door, a shocking scene awaited him. Beverley's nude body lay in plain view, her legs splayed, a nylon stocking and two handkerchiefs woven together and knotted around her neck. The cause of death wasn't strangulation, though, she'd been stabbed 22 times.

The summer of 1963 brought another break in the killings. Then, on September 8, 1963, a 58-year-old divorcee, named Evelyn Corbin, was found strangled in her home in Salem, Massachusetts. Two nylon stockings were knotted around her neck and her panties were stuffed into her mouth as a gag. Her apartment had been ransacked but valuables lying in plain sight hadn't been taken.

On November 25, while Bostonians joined the rest of the country in grieving the death of assassinated President John F. Kennedy, another murder occurred. Joann Graff was a 23-year-old industrial designer. She'd been dead three days by the time her body was found with two nylon stockings tied in an elaborate bow around her neck. There were teeth marks on her breast and there was evidence that she'd been sexually assaulted.

As detectives questioned other residents in the building, they uncovered a clue that provided a link to the Sophie Clark case. A student who lived in the apartment above Joann reported that, at around 3:25 p.m. on the day of the murder, a stranger had knocked on his door. The man was about mid-twenties with elaborately pomaded hair, dressed in dark green slacks and a dark shirt and jacket. The man asked if Joann Graff lived there (pronouncing her name incorrectly as "Joan"). The student had said no and directed the man to the correct apartment. A moment later he heard knocking from the floor below and then a door opening and closing. When a friend of Joann's phoned her 10 minutes later, there was no reply.

Just over a month later on January 4, 1964, two young women returned home to a gruesome discovery. Their roommate, 19-year-old Mary Sullivan, lay murdered, displayed in a shocking fashion. She was posed, sitting upright on a bed. Two stockings and a pink silk scarf were knotted around her neck, and a "Happy New Year" card rested against her feet. A thick liquid that looked like semen was dripping from her mouth onto her breasts. A broomstick handle had been rammed into her vagina.

The brutal murder of Mary Sullivan and the disrespectful way in which she had been posed was the last straw for Massachusetts Attorney General Edward Brooke. On January 17, 1964, he announced that he was personally taking charge of the case. In short order, Brooke ordered the formation of a task force, formally called the Special Division of Crime Research and Detection. He placed Assistant Attorney General John S. Bottomly in charge of the team, a controversial choice as Bottomly had no experience of criminal law and was universally disliked by the senior hierarchy of the Boston Police Department.

And Bottomly's first action hardly improved his standing with his police colleagues. He brought in Peter Hurkos, a controversial Dutch psychic who seemed to make a habit of involving himself in high-profile murder investigations. Hurkos had achieved some limited measure of success in the past, most notably in the Melvin Rees case, but he failed woefully in identifying the Boston Strangler. The suspect he named could be categorically cleared of involvement in any of the murders. It was a blow to Hurkos' credibility and to that of the task force.

At this point in the story, it is necessary to make a small detour, to a bizarre series of sex offenses that occurred in the Cambridge area a couple of years before the Boston Strangler appeared on the scene. Over a period of three months, a man in his late twenties took to knocking on doors and introducing himself as the representative of a modeling agency. He'd tell any woman who answered that she'd been recommended to the agency, and ask if he could measure her to ascertain that she met the agency's requirements. Many of women, flattered by the attention and interested in the money he said they could earn, allowed him to take their measurements. That done, he'd thank them, and say he'd be in touch. Of course, they never heard from him again and most of the women put it down as a harmless prank. Others, though, were offended and reported the matter to the police.

On March 17, 1961, Cambridge police apprehended a man trying to break into a house. Under questioning, the man confessed to being the "Measuring Man." He was Albert De Salvo, a 29-year-old Bostonian with numerous arrests for breaking and entering. Asked what the point of his "Measuring Man" charade was, he said it was a prank to get one over smart, high-class people. Prank or not, De Salvo's got 18 months. He was released in April 1962, two months before the first Boston Strangler murder.

In November of 1964, almost three years after his release from prison, and 11 months after the murder of Mary Sullivan, De Salvo was arrested again. This time, the charges were more serious. On

October 27, he had entered a residence and placed a knife to a woman's throat as she dozed. He tied her up and stuffed underwear in her mouth then stripped her naked and fondled her before fleeing the apartment. Before he left he apologized for what he'd done.

The woman had gotten a good look at her attacker and her description reminded the investigating officers of the Measuring Man. They brought De Salvo in, and the victim identified him from a lineup. A check with other jurisdictions turned up an interest from Connecticut. They'd had a number of similar attacks there and had given their unknown assailant the nickname, "The Green Man," because he always wore green work pants.

Faced with the accusations, De Salvo admitted to breaking into over 400 apartments and assaulting over 300 women. The police took these numbers with a pinch of salt. De Salvo was well known as a braggart with a habit of exaggerating. Nonetheless, he was in serious trouble.

De Salvo was sent to Bridgewater State Hospital for observation where his cellmate was a man named George Nassar, accused of the execution-style killing of a gas station attendant. Although he was a vicious killer, who'd previously served time for another murder, Nasser was an intelligent man. He possessed a near-genius IQ and spoke several languages. He was also known for his ability to manipulate, and at Bridgewater, he became Albert De Salvo's confidant. Not long after, Nasser placed a call to his attorney, F. Lee Bailey and Bailey took a flight from the west coast to meet with De Salvo.

No one knows why Albert De Salvo confessed to being the Boston Strangler. It has been speculated that he and Nasser cooked up a scheme whereby De Salvo would confess and Nasser would turn him in and claim the reward money, which they'd later split. De Salvo expected to go to prison for life anyway, the money would go to his wife and two kids. Another theory is that the smooth talking Nasser convinced De Salvo that there was a fortune to be made in book and movie rights. And it should also not be discounted that De Salvo was a braggart and a blowhard. The idea of being recognized as the infamous Boston Strangler must have appealed to him.

Whatever the motivation, F. Lee Bailey interviewed De Salvo at Bridgewater and then set up a meeting with Lieutenants Donovan and Sherry of the Strangler Task Force. At that meeting, he played them a tape of his interview with De Salvo, containing a confession to the Strangler murders. To the hard-pressed detectives of the Strangler task force, under increasing public and official scrutiny, De Salvo's confession must have been like manna from heaven. And there was no chance that it could be a fake. De Salvo's knowledge of the crime scenes was far too detailed, containing information that only the killer would know.

A meeting was hastily arranged between Police Commissioner McNamara, Dr. Ames Robey, the psychiatrist at Bridgewater, and De Salvo. This interview began on September 29, 1965, and resulted in more than 50 hours of tape and over 2000 pages of transcript. Again, De Salvo's detailed recollection of the crimes was impressive. Now, the police were faced with the arduous task of checking the details to make sure that De Salvo was telling the truth.

While they were doing that, De Salvo's attorney, F. Lee Bailey, sat down with Attorney General Brooke and John Bottomly, to thrash out a deal. Bailey came straight to the point. Despite De Salvo's confession, he did not believe that the State of Massachusetts had enough evidence to successfully try him as the Boston Strangler. However, De Salvo was prepared to plead guilty to the Green Man assaults, and to accept a life sentence for those crimes.

Brook and Bottomly considered their options and decided that Bailey was right. Putting De Salvo on trial constituted a huge risk, as the court proceedings would fall right in the middle of Brook's election campaign for the senate. A loss in court would seriously dent his chances. He thus agreed to Bailey's terms.

De Salvo went on trial on for the Green Man charges on January 10, 1967, and was sentenced to life in prison. However, he would serve less than seven years of his sentence.

In November 1973, while in the infirmary at Walpole State Prison, Albert De Salvo was stabbed to death by an unknown assailant. The day before his death he had placed a call to Dr. Ames Robey. De Salvo was frantic, saying he had information to share on the Boston Strangler case and that he feared for his life. Dr. Robey agreed to meet with him the next morning, but De Salvo was murdered that night. His killer has never been caught.

So was Albert De Salvo the Boston Strangler? The evidence suggests that he was not. But if that is the case, it begs the question, how could he have had such intimate knowledge of the crime scenes?

The truth is that De Salvo got as much information wrong as he got right and that most of the so-called "intimate detail" he offered was public knowledge, having been reported in the papers. It is true that he did provide some details that had been withheld from the public. But that information might easily have been fed to him, either by the real killer or by members of the Strangler task force, desperate to close the case.

Yet, even if we assume that De Salvo gained most of his knowledge by following the case in the newspapers, how could he, a man of below average intelligence, memorize that much detail?

It turns out that De Salvo had a near photographic memory, as testified to by his lawyers Jon Asgeirsson and Tony Troy.

Then there's the issue of victim profiles. Serial killers most often target victims that are of similar type. Yet, in the Boston Strangler case, there are two distinct victim groups, one young, one old. This seems to indicate two separate killers.

But might one of those killers not be De Salvo? Let's consider for a while the Green Man assaults, which started in the midst of the Boston Strangler's murderous campaign. Is it likely that Albert De Salvo could have been, simultaneously, a vicious murderer, and a man who tied up his victims, fondled them and then fled the scene after apologizing for what he'd done? It seems highly unlikely.

All of the above is, of course, circumstantial, but there is physical evidence, too, that exonerates De Salvo, at least in one of the murders. For years, both the De Salvo and Sullivan families fought for the bodies of De Salvo and of Mary Sullivan to be exhumed and for the evidence gathered from the scene to be put through DNA analysis. When this was eventually granted, in 2001, it proved two things; that Sullivan did not die in the way De Salvo described in his confession, and that whoever raped Mary Sullivan, it wasn't Albert De Salvo.

Which leaves us with the question: Who was the Boston Strangler? In all likelihood, the Boston Strangler did not exist, at least not as the serial slayer of 13 women. The evidence suggests at least two killers, one targeting older women, one younger. Some of the murders might not even have been connected to either series.

As to who any of these men might have been, the best evidence we have are the eyewitness descriptions of the man seen near both the Clark and Graff murder scenes. Those eyewitnesses were brought to view De Salvo while he was incarcerated at Bridgewater. Both of them categorically said that De Salvo wasn't the man they'd seen. In fact, they said, the man more closely resembled De Salvo's cellmate, George Nasser.

The Frankford Slasher

Frankford is an ethnically diverse working-class neighborhood of Philadelphia, which actually predates the city itself. Traditionally a manufacturing center, the area later became famous as the winter headquarters for a number of traveling circuses. At one stage, the neighborhood boasted a symphony orchestra, and it was also the birthplace of the Philadelphia Eagles football team. In 1922, The El (elevated train) arrived, bringing with it prosperity and jobs, as Frankford was absorbed into the larger city of Philadelphia.

But by 1980, the 13-block strip that lay in the El's shadow along Frankford Avenue had devolved into a crime-ridden slum frequented by prostitutes and drug addicts. Sylvester Stallone selected this rundown area as a location for his 1976 Academy Award winning picture, Rocky. But in the mid-eighties, the area acquired a less desirable claim to fame. It became the hunting ground for a brutal serial killer known as the Frankford Slasher.

The Slasher first came to public attention on August 26, 1985. At around 8.30 am on that morning, transit workers discovered the body of a woman lying between the rows of railroad ties at the SEPTA train yard at Penn and Bridge Streets.

The victim was nude from the waist down and had been posed in a sexually provocative position, with her legs spread and her blouse pulled up to expose her breasts. She'd suffered multiple stab wounds to the head and chest and there was also a vicious slash across her abdomen, which was deep enough to expose her internal organs. An autopsy would reveal that she'd been raped.

An identification followed the next day. The victim was 52-year-old Helen Patent, a resident of Parkland, Pennsylvania, in nearby Bucks County. Patent was divorced but still shared a home with her former husband, Kermit, who claimed that she'd had left the week before without saying where she was going. This was not unusual, he explained, as they lived separate lives.

As police canvassed the area, they learned that Helen Patent frequented many of the bars along Frankford Avenue. It looked as though she might have met a stranger in one of those establishments and ended up being raped and murdered. Such incidents of random violence are unfortunately all too common in any big city.

Except, this wasn't random. On January 3, 1986, police were called to the scene of another brutal homicide, just ten miles from where Helen Patent's body had been found. The victim was 68-year-old Anna Carroll, and she'd been killed in her own apartment. She was found lying on the floor of her bedroom, six deep knife wounds to her back. Her killer had also ripped her abdomen open, the wound running from groin to breastbone as though he was trying to gut her. A bloody kitchen knife, the likely weapon, lay nearby.

Given the short time between the two incidents, the wounds inflicted on the bodies and the fact that both Patent and Carroll had been regulars on the Frankford bar scene, it might have been reasonable to assume that the two murders were connected. But the police didn't initially investigate them as such, treating them instead as unrelated incidents.

Nearly a year passed without progress in either of the investigations. Then, on Christmas Day 1986, a neighbor of 64-year-old Susan Olszef, noticed her front door standing open and, on investigation, found Olszef lying on the floor with six knife wounds in her back.

Olszef's apartment was on Richmond Avenue, some three miles from the first murder scene and the police soon learned that she, like the first two victims, also frequented the Frankford area bars. In fact, all three women had been regulars at the Golden Bar (known locally as "Goldie's"), situated on the 5200 block of Frankford Avenue, near the elevated train terminal.

The Goldie's connection at least provided investigators with a line of inquiry they could follow. However, that proved easier said than done. The Frankford Street area attracted commuters from all over the city, traveling on the El to frequent the late night bars and taverns. It would be easy for an anonymous murderer to ride in, commit his crime and then lose himself in the crowds before leaving the area in a car or on the El. Further hampering the investigation was that the police still did not yet believe that the three murders were the work of a serial killer. Then the fourth victim turned up.

Jeanne Durkin, 28, was a street person who usually occupied the doorway of an abandoned bakery, two buildings away from Goldie's Bar. On January 8, 1987, a restaurant employee found her lying beneath a storage truck parked on a Pratt Street lot. This was just a block away from where Helen Patent's body had been discovered. Durkin had been stabbed in the chest, buttocks and back (an autopsy would record 74 wounds). She was naked from the waist down, posed in a spread-eagled position. The attack had been so frenzied that blood was liberally spattered against a fence and the side of the truck.

It was now clear to all but the police that Philadelphia had another serial killer on its hands, to go with the recent high profile cases of Gary Heidnik and Harrison Graham. Under increasing pressure from both the public and the media, the authorities hastily assembled a task force to look into the Frankford homicides.

They began by canvassing the patrons and staff of Frankford's many bars, garnering lots of advice and conjecture but few solid leads. One thing did emerge, though, about the fourth victim, Jeanne Durkin. Those who knew Durkin insisted that she would not have been easily overcome. Durkin had been living on the streets for five years, in between spells in various mental institutions. She was streetwise and independent. The police heard of an incident in which six officers had tried, unsuccessfully, to subdue her. This led investigators to believe that she must have known her attacker.

An early suspect was a woman named Michelle Dehner, who had argued with Durkin over a blanket the night before her death, but further investigation cleared Dehner of any involvement. The police were back to square one, back to the belief that the murders were unrelated. Over the next year, they'd have cause to rethink that position.

The next Frankford Slasher victim was Margaret Vaughan, 66, found in the foyer of an apartment building on November 11, 1988. Vaughn had, in fact, had an apartment in the building until recently, when she'd been evicted for unpaid rent. She'd been stabbed 29 times.

But at least, this time, police had something to work on. On the
night of her death, Vaughan had been drinking in a local bar. She
had been in the company of a Caucasian man, who was described
as having a round face and glasses and walking with a limp. Based
on the witness accounts, a sketch artist produced a likeness, which
was broadly distributed, but produced no results.

Then on January 19, 1989, the killer struck again. Theresa
Sciortino, aged 30, was found in her apartment on Arrott Street.
She was lying on her back in the kitchen, in a pool of blood,
wearing only a pair of white socks. Her attacker had used a large
knife to inflict twenty-five deep slashes across her face, arms, and
chest. He'd also used a three-foot piece of wood to sexually assault
her. A bloodstained knife was found at the scene and the killer had
also left behind a bloody footprint. Blood was spattered
everywhere, indicating that Theresa had put up a fierce fight for
her life.

Police inquiries turned up a number of similarities to the other
murders. Sciortino's apartment was close to both Frankford
Avenue and several of the other crime scenes. She was a regular at
various bars along the strip and was known to regularly bring men
home from those bars. Like Jean Durkin, she'd done time in mental
institutions and was currently a psychiatric outpatient. On the
night of her death, she had been drinking at the Jolly Post Tavern,
in the company of a middle-aged white man. She left with the man
at about 6:00 in the evening. Shortly after, her neighbor had heard
a scuffle in her apartment.

Some of these leads looked promising. But, as in the other cases,
they inevitably led nowhere. The police increased their presence
on the ground in Frankford and braced for another murder. They
didn't have long to wait.

At around 2:00 on the morning of April 29, 1990, an officer patrolling along Frankford Avenue discovered a nude female body, in an alley behind Newman's Seafood Market. Her head and face had been severely battered and she had been viciously stabbed 36 times in the face, neck, chest, and back. In addition, her stomach was ripped open, allowing her intestines to spill through a gaping wound, and her left nipple was either cut or bitten off. There were also defensive wounds to her hands and arms.

The victim was identified as 46-year-old Cathy Dowd. She lived nearby and had been seen walking with an older white man just a few hours before her death. The police suspected that this might be the same man who had been seen with both Vaughn and Sciortino, but as they began questioning employees of the fish market, a new suspect emerged.

Leonard Christopher bore no resemblance to the elusive white man. In fact, he was African American. But, after admitting that he knew one of the earlier victims, Margaret Vaughan, the police became suspicious. And that suspicion intensified when Christopher offered an alibi for the time of the murder that turned out to be a lie. Then, a witness came forward to say that Dowd and Christopher had been drinking together in a bar on the night of her death. Another witness testified that she'd seen him emerging from the alley with a large knife tucked into his belt.

A search of his apartment turned up clothing with blood on it, and although a viable reason was offered for this (his boss testified that he'd instructed Christopher to clean up the blood left in the alley), Christopher was placed under arrest.

But if the police believed that they finally had their man, they were mistaken. On September 6, 1990, while Leonard Christopher was in prison awaiting trial, the Frankford Slasher struck again. Michelle Dehner had been a suspect in the Durkin murder, now she was a victim herself.

Detectives called to the scene that Saturday afternoon, found her lying on the floor of her apartment. She'd been stabbed 23 times, the wounds concentrated on her chest and stomach. There was no sign of forced entry and no weapon was found at the scene. It did not escape police attention that the murder was committed in close proximity to the others and that Michelle Dehner (known locally as "Crazy Michelle") had frequented the same bars as the other victims.

With this latest murder, word on the street was that the police had arrested the wrong man and there were calls for Leonard Christopher to be released. Nonetheless, he remained in custody until his trial, which began on November 29, 1990.

Christopher's defense attorney made great capital of the series of murders, in particular the one committed while Christopher was in custody. No doubt, he hoped that it would create a reasonable doubt in the minds of the jury and, in truth, the case against Christopher seemed tenuous at best. There was no physical evidence linking him to the crime scene and no one could testify that they'd seen him commit the murder. He had no history of violence, no motive. Several witnesses testified that Christopher was a likable, mild-mannered man. He didn't seem the type.

But it wasn't quite as simple as that. Christopher's behavior in the aftermath of the murder had aroused police suspicion for a reason. For starters, on the morning of the murder, he'd told his boss,

Jaesa Phang, that a white woman of about forty-five years old had been murdered in the alley when the police had not yet revealed those details to anyone. A few days later, he'd made a strange comment to Phang: "Maybe I killed her." Then, in an apparent effort to deflect suspicion, he'd reported to police that he'd seen a white man on the street at 1:00 am, even though none of the other witnesses had seen such a man.

Jaesa Phang also testified that, in the week following the murder, Christopher had been in a constant state of agitation. He said that he had seen a white man kill Carol Dowd and was certain that the man would now kill him, to stop him talking. When the police found a bloodstained tissue that proved to have Type O (Dowd's blood type) in a driveway next to Christopher's apartment building, he suddenly remembered seeing a white man drop it there on the night of the murder. The problem was, according to Christopher's own testimony, he was not home that night.

These obvious lies would count against him. On December 12, after 8 hours of deliberation, split over two days, the jury returned their verdict. They found Leonard Christopher guilty of the murder of Carol Dowd. He was sentenced to life in prison.

With the conviction of Leonard Christopher, the Carol Dowd murder case was officially closed. But what of the other seven murders? Is it possible that Christopher was responsible for those killings too?

On the face of it, it appears most unlikely. Many questions remain regarding the quality of evidence used to convict Christopher. In fact, he was convicted largely on the basis of his behavior in the wake of the Dowd murder. Taking into account that, if he were the Frankford Slasher, the Dowd murder would have been his seventh, would he have been likely to behave in such an agitated fashion? Would his behavior not have been noticed after the earlier murders?

But, if Leonard Christopher wasn't the Frankford Slasher, who was? And why did he suddenly stop after the Michelle Dehner murder?

We may never know the answers to those questions. When a series of murders stops without the perpetrator being caught it is usually due to the killer dying, leaving the area, or being incarcerated for some other crime. Any of those fates may have befallen the Slasher. Either way, it appears he got away with murder.

Bible John

Glasgow, Scotland's largest city and economic heartbeat, has produced its fair share of villains. From Madeleine Smith who poisoned her lover in 1857 and was acquitted under the unique Scottish verdict of Not Proven, to Dr. Edward William Pritchard who committed a similar crime on his wife in 1865 and was the last man to be publically executed in Scotland; from the homicidal butler, Archibald Hall, to the notorious serial killer Peter Manuel, slayer of eight people in a murderous spree during the fifties. And then there's Ian Brady, born in Glasgow, who gained infamy for the horrendous Moors Murders.

But one serial killer, largely unknown outside Scotland, has entered the realm of Glasgow folklore, someone that Glaswegian parents still use as a bogeyman to get children to behave. He is Bible John, a still unidentified serial killer who terrorized the city during the late 1960's.

The fiend made his public debut on the night of February 22, 1968. Patricia Docker was a young nurse, the mother of a young toddler, whose husband was a Royal Air Force corporal stationed in England. On that Thursday evening some of Patricia's friends were going to the over 25's night at the Barrowland Ballroom, one of Glasgow's popular nightspots. They persuaded her to join them for a night of dancing and fun. Patricia's parents encouraged her to go along, she worked so hard, after all, she could do with letting her hair down for an evening.

Leaving her young son in the care of his grandparents Patricia set off for the nightclub, stopping off first at another dancehall, the Majestic. Few people remember seeing Patricia at the Barrowland that evening. Some witnesses later recalled seeing her at both dancehalls, but couldn't say who she spoke to or who her dance partners might have been. However, more than one witness did recall that she left in the company of a young man.

The following morning, Friday the 23rd, a man on his way to work noticed something lying at the side of a quiet lane on his route. On closer examination, he was horrified to find it was the naked body of a young woman. The man ran immediately to call the police.

Officers arriving at the scene soon determined that the woman had been strangled with her own pantyhose and had been dead for several hours. An autopsy would later reveal that she'd also been raped. The police began searching the immediate area for the woman's clothing and other effects. But their efforts turned up nothing, leaving them to theorize that she had been killed somewhere else before being dumped in the lane.

By now, a crowd had gathered and someone was able to identify the victim. She was Patricia Docker they said, she lived close by. The bystander then ran to call Patricia's parents who were faced with the unenviable task of identifying their daughter's body, which had been left just yards away from their house.

While the police canvassed the neighborhood, they also continued their search for Patricia's clothes and handbag, even sending divers into the icy waters of the nearby River Cart. They found nothing, although the bag would later be retrieved from the River Clyde, suggesting that the killer was from that part of the city.

Neither did questioning the neighbors provide many answers. One woman did say that she'd heard cries in the early morning hours, but the information was too vague to be of use. A photograph of a policewoman of similar stature to Patricia, and wearing similar clothes, was circulated in the hope was that it might stir someone's memory. It too, led nowhere. Before long the trail had gone cold.

A year and a half passed and the brutal murder of Patricia Docker had faded from the memory of most Glaswegians when the killer struck again.

On the evening of August 16, 1969, Jemima McDonald, a 32-year-old mother of three, was looking forward to an evening out. With her sister, Margaret, babysitting her kids for the evening, Jemima headed for the Barrowland. As was common with young women of the day, she wore her hair in curlers under a scarf. On arriving at the club, she immediately headed for the bathroom where she removed the curlers and freshened up her makeup before making for the dance floor.

Jemima danced almost exclusively with one partner that night, a tall, fair-haired man in his late 20s or early 30s, wearing a blue suit. The couple was seen together in the early hours of the following morning, walking away from the dancehall.

Margaret was perplexed when her sister didn't show up to collect her children by the morning of August 17. But as the day wore on, she became more and more concerned. Later that day Margaret heard talk in the neighborhood about a body that some kids had discovered in an old tenement building in nearby MacKeith Street. Fearing the worst, she walked to the building where she made a grisly discovery.

Unlike Patricia, Jemima was fully clothed. However, like the earlier victim, she had been strangled with her own nylons and her handbag was missing from the scene. She'd also been beaten and raped. As the police began looking into similarities between the two homicides they discovered another connection. Both Patricia and Jemima had been menstruating at the time they were killed.

With not much evidence discovered at the crime scene, the police moved on to their next priority, questioning those who'd been at the Barrowland on the night Jemima was killed. When this failed to turn up any useful leads, they staged a re-enactment. A policewoman who resembled Jemima was dressed in similar clothing and retraced Jemima's last known steps. This yielded a few clues but got the police no closer to identifying a particular suspect.

They did, however, have a description of the man who'd been in Jemima's company that evening. A rough sketch was created and circulated to the media, the first time this had ever occurred in a Scottish murder investigation - sketches of suspects had previously been for police use only.

Meanwhile, Jemima's six siblings offered a reward of £100 for information leading to an arrest. This too, produced no tangible results.

The elusive killer had waited 18 months between the murders of Patricia Docker and Jemima McDonald. He'd wait just two months before claiming his next victim.

On Oct. 30, 1969, 20-year-old Helen Puttock was planning an evening out at the Barrowland Ballroom with her sister, Jean. Her husband offered to stay home to look after their two young boys, but he warned his wife to be careful. The murder of Jemima McDonald was still fresh in the public's mind. Helen scoffed at his concerns. She and Jean would be together all night, she was confident they would be safe.

During the evening, Helen began dancing with a tall, young man and, according to Jean's later testimony, the two spent much of the evening in each other's company. At around midnight, Helen told her new friend that she and Jean had to leave. He offered to see them home in a taxi.

The police would later question Jean extensively about the short cab ride. She said that the man seemed to resent her presence and had addressed himself solely to Helen during the cab ride. However, she had learned that the man's name was John Templeton or Sempleson, that he had a sister and had been raised in a strict religious household and was adept at quoting passages of scripture. He spoke disparagingly of the sort of women who frequented places like the Barrowland, calling the dancehall a "den of iniquity." Somewhere during the conversation, John had also mentioned that he had a cousin who had recently hit a hole-in-one while playing golf.

When the cab had dropped Jean off at her house in Knightswood, John had not even bothered to acknowledge her as she said goodbye. As the cab pulled away from the curb, Jean had no idea that it would be the last time she saw her sister.

The following morning, Helen's body was discovered in the back garden of her flat in Earl Street, Scotstoun. As with the previous victims, she'd been strangled with her own pantyhose and her handbag had been taken. She had also been having her period, and the killer had removed her sanitary napkin and placed it in one of her armpits. An autopsy would show that she'd been raped, but unlike in the other crimes, the killer had left a couple of clues; a bite mark on the victim's leg and a semen stain on her clothing. These did not help police at the time, but would come into play decades later.

As the police launched a massive investigation, one of the biggest in Scottish history, the press picked up on the killer's apparent ability to quote scripture and gave him a nickname that would haunt Glasgow for decades to come: "Bible John."

But who was Bible John? Did he even exist or was he purely a media creation. At least one of the lead investigators on the case believed that the murders were unconnected and unlikely to have been committed by the same man. This is a startling viewpoint given the similarities between the crimes; all of the victims had spent the last night of their lives at the Barrowland Ballroom; all three were strangled with their own nylons; each of the bodies was left in close proximity to the victim's home; the handbags of all three victims were carried away by the killer; all three victims were menstruating at the time of their deaths. Victims two and three had been in the company of a tall, fair-haired man. It seems highly unlikely that they were unconnected.

Over 100 officers were now working the case, collecting more than 50, 000 statements, questioning bus and taxi drivers, even going undercover at the Barrowland. A color sketch of the man seen with both Jemima and Helen was released, while the BBC screened a recreation of Helen's last known movements. Jean's description led police to focus part of their investigation on the armed forces, as Bible John's short haircut may have indicated that he was serving in the military.

Additionally, the police began questioned dentists about male patients who had the overlapping tooth that Jean had described. And the police even visited golf courses, up and down the country, to check on John's story about his cousin's hole-in-one.

Meanwhile, a Glasgow newspaper brought in a renowned Dutch psychic, and a local psychiatrist produced a profile of sorts, describing Bible John as friendly, but somewhat prudish with an interest in subjects ranging from the Third Reich to sorcery. Helen's husband even put up a reward for information, amounting to his entire life's savings. It was all to no avail. Over the years, Jean would pay over 250 visits to view suspects that matched her description. None of them was Bible John.

Time passed, and with no arrest or even progress to report the case began to fade from the public eye. In 1977, a murder that bore some of the hallmarks of the Bible John murders, briefly stirred renewed interest in the case.

In 1983, a wealthy Glaswegian hired a private detective to track down a childhood friend whom he thought resembled an artist's depiction of Bible John. The investigators found the man in question living in Holland. He was questioned but quickly cleared of any involvement.

But the police were not without suspects, and one, in particular, stood out. The man, known as John McInnes, bore an uncanny resemblance to the police sketch. Even after he committed suicide in 1980, he continued to be considered a prime suspect.

By the late 1990s, DNA technology allowed the police to revisit the evidence, in particular, the semen left on Helen's clothing. In February 1996, Marie Cassidy of Glasgow University supervised the exhumation of John McInnes's body and took DNA samples for comparison to the evidence. The results proved conclusively that John McInnes was not Bible John.

Another possible suspect was the serial killer Peter Tobin, convicted in 2007 of the murder of student Angelika Kluk. Tobin had lived in Glasgow at the time of the Bible John murders and bore a strong resemblance to the suspect. He was also a regular at the Barrowland, and at least one woman testified that she had been raped by Tobin after meeting him at the dancehall. There are other pieces of circumstantial evidence that point to Tobin as well.

All three of his former wives testified that they had been strangled and raped by him. They also said that Tobin was often driven to violence by the menstrual cycle, something which has long been considered the motive behind the Bible John murders. Tobin was also a staunch Roman Catholic with strong religious views.

A DNA comparison could have proven conclusively whether Tobin was Bible John or no, but unfortunately, the DNA evidence had become degraded by the time of his arrest, making such a comparison impossible.

We will likely never know who Bible John was.

The Servant Girl Annihilator

On New Year's Eve, 1884, a murder occurred in the city of Austin, Texas. The crime was brutal and bloody, eliciting an outraged editorial in the city's newspaper, the Austin Statesman. "Bloody Work!" read the headline in that publication, competing for attention with local interest stories, opinion pieces, fashions, and social announcements. The good citizens of Austin read, expressed shock, and then went about their business. The victim, after all, was only a Negro servant, the crime more than likely the result of some squabble.

Mollie Smith had kept house and cooked for Mr. and Mrs. William Hall on West Pecan Street. Mollie, 25-years-old at the time of her death, lived with a male companion in a room at the back of the Halls' two-story home. She was killed behind the house, found lying in the snow, her head gashed, face badly bludgeoned. Her nightdress had been torn to shreds and it appeared, from the way she was posed, that she'd been raped.

Walter Spencer, Mollie's common-law husband, had been attacked as well, a deep gash running across his face. Under questioning, Walter said that he'd woken in terrible pain, the room in disarray and blood spattered, Mollie gone. He went immediately to look for help, rousing William Hall from sleep. Hall had then followed a blood trail through the snow and discovered Mollie's corpse.

As someone went to call the Marshall, Hall conducted a search of the premises and discovered a bloodstained axe, presumably the murder weapon. He also noticed a bloody handprint on the wall.

Marshall Grooms Lee had arrived in the meantime, bringing a team of bloodhounds with him. The dogs were dispatched to track the killer but fresh snow had fallen in the interim and the trail was soon lost.

No matter, there was an obvious suspect in this case, a man named William "Lem" Brooks, whom Mollie had once been involved with. Quite obviously, Brooks was jealous at Mollie's new relationship with Spencer and had exacted revenge. The blood spatters in the room, reaching almost to the ceiling in places, attested to a level of violence that could only have come from a crime of passion. Despite protesting his innocence and providing an alibi, Brooks was arrested. An inquest would determine whether there was sufficient evidence to put him on trial.

In those days, with few, if any, forensic techniques available to law officers, courts relied primarily on eyewitness testimony, confessions, and "common sense" based on circumstantial evidence. Thus it was that the six white men making up the coroner's jury decided that Lem Brooks should be held for trial. He had the means and motive after all, and his alibi witnesses were probably lying to cover for him.

However, the charges against Brooks were dropped before the matter came to trial, and with no other suspects or clues to follow, the murder of Mollie Smith was quickly forgotten.

Then, on Wednesday, May 6, another woman was killed, the manner of her death startlingly similar to that of Mollie Smith.

The victim's name was Eliza Shelley, and she worked as a cook to former state legislator, Dr. L.B. Johnson. She and her three children occupied a cabin behind the Johnson family home. On the night of the murder, Mrs. Johnson heard shouts coming from Eliza's cabin and sent her niece to investigate. The girl returned in a state of shock and reported what she'd seen. Dr. Johnson then went to the cabin himself and found 30-year-old Eliza Shelley dead on the floor.

She had been stabbed in the head with a sharp implement, and there was a gaping wound to her skull that appeared to have been made by an axe. The killer had struck her so hard that he'd cleaved the skull in two, exposing the brain matter. Blood-soaked pillows suggested that she had been attacked while she slept and then dragged onto the floor. The condition of her nightdress, pulled up to expose her nude body, led Dr. Johnson to believe that she'd been raped. The weapon had been removed from the scene and the only other clue was a set of footprints, large and broad leading to and from the cottage, suggesting that a large, shoeless man had committed the crime.

Eliza's eight-year-old son described a man entering the cabin in the middle of the night. The boy said that the man had shoved him into a corner, thrown a blanket over his head and told him to be quiet. He'd apparently fallen asleep soon after (it was speculated that he might have been chloroformed, as a bottle of that substance had recently had been stolen from a dentist's home).

Eliza's two younger brothers, who slept in the same bed with their mother, were unable to add anything more.

The Marshall was sent for and again dispatched his bloodhounds, which were unable to pick up a trail. Nevertheless, Marshall Lee quickly secured the arrest of a dimwitted, 19-year-old boy, found wandering around barefoot nearby. However, when the tracks were measured again his feet, it was clear that he was not the person who made them. He was released from custody at around the same time that another black man was arrested. He too would soon be released, as the next attack, occurring as it did while he was incarcerated, proved his innocence.

On May 23, just over two weeks after the murder of Eliza Shelley, another black servant was attacked and killed. Irene Cross lived in a cottage, across the street from a beer garden. On the night of the murder someone broke in and attacked Irene with a knife, the assault so vicious that it appeared as though the murderer was trying to remove her scalp. In addition, her arm was so badly slashed that it was nearly severed from her body.

Because of the slightly different modus operandi and the choice of weapon, no one initially linked this murder to the series. Prevailing wisdom held that the influx of foreign workers was to blame. Most white people held the belief that a black man was responsible, while the black population was quietly seething at the perceived lack of effort to solve the murders of black servants. Three women had been brutally slain and yet no one was in custody.

Three months passed. Then, in late August, another horrific murder. Rebecca Ramey lived on San Jacinto and Cedar Streets, a block south of where Eliza Shelley had been killed. She was in the employ of Valentine Weed, a livery stable owner. On that balmy August night, someone entered Rebecca's home and knocked both her and her 11-year-old daughter, Mary, unconscious. Mary was dragged outside, raped, and then stabbed through both ears with an iron rod. She died at the scene. Rebecca survived the attack but was unable to remember anything that might help to apprehend the murderer.

This latest murder had the city of Austin in an uproar. People wanted the killer caught and brought to justice. Granted, the killer appeared to be targeting black servants, and that gave the white middle and upper classes some measure of security. But the latest victim had been a child. Everyone was of one mind in demanding action from the police. Many voices raised concerns about Marshall Lee's competence to do the job.

Then, a month after the Ramsey murder, the killer emerged again, this time taking two victims in a single night.

On September 26, Lucinda Boddy, a cook in a home near the university, went to visit her friend Gracie Vance. Gracie lived in a servant's cabin behind the house of her employer, Major W. D. Dunham. Her common-law husband, Orange Washington, lived with her. Lucinda passed an uneventful day in the company of her friends. Then, as darkness fell, Gracie invited her to spend the night and she readily agreed.

At around midnight, Lucinda was awakened by Gracie screaming. She saw Orange spring from the bed and then immediately collapse as a dark figure struck him with something. Then she herself was hit in the head. Dazed by the hefty blow, she felt herself being dragged across the floor, her clothes being ripped. Then she blacked out.

When Lucinda regained consciousness it was dark and quiet in the cabin. She staggered to her feet and found a kerosene lantern, using it to look around. Orange lay still on the floor, an ugly, gaping wound to his head. There was another man in the room. "Don't look at me!" he spat, before commanding her to put the lamp out. Lucinda wasn't about to comply. She threw the lamp at the man and ran, screaming for help.

Her screams alerted Major Dunham, who came from the house holding a gun.

"We're all dead!" Lucinda screamed before collapsing.

Smelling kerosene fumes Dunham ran for the cabin where he spotted Orange Washington lying on the floor, an axe beside him. Gracie was nowhere to be seen.

Aware of the recent attacks on black servants, the major walked to the boundary of his property and called out to one of his neighbors for help. It was then that he came across Gracie's body. Her head had been crushed and there was a blood-covered brick nearby. It was also clear that she'd been sexually assaulted.

Orange Washington succumbed to his wounds the following day, bringing to five the number of victims killed by the mysterious intruder. Except that there were now doubts as to how many attackers were involved. Lucinda Boddy's evidence seemed to suggest that two men had carried out these latest murders.

After the last attack, the citizens of Austin demanded that drastic measures be taken. Some called for the formation of vigilance committees, others suggested questioning every stranger in town, still others wanted all suspicious persons run out. One opinion was near universal, though, most everyone agreed that Marshal Lee was not up to the job of catching the killer.

Lee responded to this criticism by arresting two new suspects, Dock Woods and Oliver Townsend, both black men who lived in the area. Lucinda Boddy had apparently named Woods as the man she'd seen in the cabin and he was known to have harassed Gracie in the past. Townsend had been overheard by a witness, threatening to kill Gracie. In addition, when arrested, Woods had in his possession, a bloody shirt.

Eventually though, both men had to be released due to lack of evidence and Lee turned his attention to another suspect. Walter Spencer had been assaulted along with the first victim, Mollie Smith. Now he found himself under arrest as a suspect. He would eventually be tried and acquitted.

So far, the murders had followed a familiar pattern: the black servants of well-to-do employers, attacked in their homes in the middle of the night; victims bludgeoned to death with some or other implement, women raped. Yet for all this, few believed that the same perpetrator was responsible. When Prosecutor E.T. Moore suggested such a theory, his law enforcement colleagues laughed it off. They believed that the murders were the result of unrelated disputes between black people. They were soon to be savagely disabused of that theory.

The fiend whom the Austin Statesman had by now labeled the "Servant Girl Annihilator" struck again on Christmas Eve, 1885. On that evening, Moses Hancock and his wife Susan had attended a concert at the State Institution for the Blind. On returning, Mrs. Hancock had retired to bed, while Moses sat up a while, eventually dozing off in a chair. Some time later, he woke and discovered that his wife was not in bed. Conducting a frantic search of the house he found her eventually lying in the backyard. She had been bludgeoned with an axe, her head cleaved open, exposing her brain. Blood ran from her ears and matted in her hair. It was also evident that she had been raped.

Marshal Lee had by now been ousted from his position but his successor, James Lucy, stuck to the tried and tested method and brought in the bloodhounds. The handlers set about trying to pick up a trail, but they'd barely got started when word came of another murder.

The second victim was Eula Phillips, a member of Austin's social elite and broadly regarded as one of the "loveliest women in town." Eula lived with her husband, Jimmy, and their infant son, in one of Austin's wealthiest neighborhoods. Her nude body was discovered in an alley close to her home. She lay spread-eagled, with her arms pinned under some lumber, leading some to believe that two men must have carried out the crime. Jimmy, too, had been attacked. He was found in his own bed, knocked unconscious, a severe wound to his head. The boy lay next to him, unharmed. A bloody axe was discarded in the middle of the floor and a trail of blood ran from the bedroom to the alley where Eula was found, her skull smashed in. A shoe print in blood was left behind on the porch.

The following day, Austin's printing presses went into overdrive. "The Demons have transferred their thirst for blood to white people!" screamed one of the papers. "Blood! Blood! Blood!" was the headline in another.

And the hysteria created by the papers soon transferred to the populace at large. There was a run on guns and ammunition, while a citizen's meeting attended by over 500 resulted in a resolution to erect "moonlight towers" to better illuminate the streets (these are still in place, over a century later).

Meanwhile, Marshal Lucy hired and posted more officers, and rewards were offered by both the governor, and a citizen's group. Detectives and bounty hunters arrived from all over the country to cash in, while extra security precautions put a damper on many a Christmas celebration.

A pall fell over the city, a morbid expectancy that the papers would soon be trumpeting a new series of atrocities. Yet, Christmas and New Year passed without incident. Then, out of the blue, a new development emerged as a couple of arrests were made in quick succession.

The arrests made little sense and seemed entirely devoid of supporting evidence, yet Moses Hancock and Jimmy Phillips, husbands of the two murdered women, were taken into custody and charged with their murders. The theory went something like this: each man had wanted to do away with his spouse and so had decided to murder them in a way that made them appear part of the series of 'servant girl' attacks.

Putting aside the absurdity of two men coincidentally deciding, on that same night, to murder their wives in exactly the same manner, the DA decided to press forward with the trials.

In the case of Moses Hancock, the state alleged that a letter found in a trunk at the Hancock house was motive for the murder. In the letter, Susan Hancock had written that she was considering leaving her husband because of his drinking.   The DA alleged that Moses had read the letter, gotten drunk, and then killed his wife in a frenzy. The trial resulted in a hung jury, and Hancock walked free.

The Phillips case was somewhat more salacious. It was alleged that Eula Phillips was unhappy in her marriage and that she been prostituting herself at a "house of assignation." Phillips had found out and killed her in a rage. Testimony was entered about Eula's affairs with other men, including prominent local politicians. The jury also heard that Jimmy Phillips had once threatened his wife with a knife and that Eula was afraid of him.

Jimmy's father brought in a crack team of lawyers and, for the most part, they managed to show up the DA's evidence for what it was, a hodge-podge of supposition and innuendo. Still, the jury found sufficient cause to convict Jimmy Phillips of second-degree murder. He was sentenced to seven years, a verdict later overturned by the Texas Court of Appeals. Neither he nor Moses Hancock was ever re-tried.

There were no more murders after those of Susan Hancock and Eula Phillips. Many suspects have been considered in the ensuing decades, but the identity of the "Servant Girl Annihilator" remains a mystery that will probably never be solved.

Jack The Stripper

Duke's Meadows, on the banks of the River Thames in Chiswick, West London, was well known to the police as a spot favored by prostitutes for servicing their clients. It was called locally by the crude nickname, "Gobbler's Gulch," and the constables who routinely patrolled the area were quite used to finding the paths littered with discarded prophylactics. But, on the early morning of June 17, 1959, a somewhat more shocking discovery awaited them. A woman sat propped up against a small willow tree, her dress torn open to expose her breasts and the scratches on her throat. She had been strangled.

The victim was identified as Elizabeth Figg, a prostitute who also used the street name, Ann Phillips. Initial enquiries ruled out her pimp boyfriend, a Trinidadian boxer named Fenton "Baby" Ward, and the investigation pretty much ground to a halt after that. Even in that relatively non-violent era, prostitute murders were not uncommon. Elizabeth Figg was soon forgotten. It would be four years before anyone would have cause to mention her name again.

Gwynneth Rees had a lot in common with Elizabeth Figg. Like Figg, she'd come to London in her teens, looking for a more glamorous existence than her small hometown in South Wales offered. Like Figg, she soon drifted into the twilight world of prostitution. Like Figg, she ended up dead, her strangled body discovered on a garbage dump alongside the Thames on November 8, 1963. Rees had last been seen getting into a car with a man on September 29. A post-mortem would reveal that she'd been strangled with a ligature and that several of her teeth had been knocked out. She also had a sexually transmitted disease, an occupational hazard for 'working girls' in an era when many clients refused to wear condoms.

As the police looked into Gwynneth Rees' background, they found no shortage of suspects, chief among them her pimp, Cornelius "Connie" Whitehead. A violent criminal with links to the notorious Kray Twins, Whitehead was known to deliver savage beatings to his girls. Rees had recently run away from him and he was known to be looking for her.

Another theory was that Rees might have died as the result of an illegal abortion, but that didn't tally with the evidence. Presuming that the abortionist had to dispose of her body, why leave it where it was sure to be discovered? And why strangle her? Before long, the Rees case, like the Figg case before it, had gone cold. The public had very little interest in a couple of murdered prostitutes, and the police, therefore, had very little incentive for prioritizing the case.

But then another prostitute turned up dead.

Hanna Tailford was from a mining town in the Northeast of England. As a child, she was known for her disruptive behavior and had been expelled from several schools. As a teenager, she ran away to London, where she was soon involved in prostitution, with a sideline in petty theft.

On February 2, 1964, rowers on the Thames found Tailford's naked body floating in the river near Hammersmith Bridge. She'd been strangled and several of her teeth were missing. Her semen-stained panties had been stuffed into her mouth. Hannah Tailford was 30-years-old at the time of her death and had been working as a prostitute for over a decade. It was an ugly end to a joyless existence.

Although the Tailford murder bore obvious similarities to the Figg and Rees cases, the police had not yet flagged it as a series. Instead, their investigation focused on the sordid world that Hannah Tailford inhabited, a world of pornography and society sex parties. Tailford was known to have appeared in underground "stag films." She was also fond of sharing stories about the bizarre orgies she'd been paid to participate in. On one occasion she'd attended an orgy at the home of a French diplomat, on another, she'd been paid £25 to have sex with a man in a gorilla costume, while a crowd of upper-crust revelers cheered them on.

Might Tailford have been silenced by someone with connections to this sleazy world? The police seemed to think so. They interviewed hundreds of people who they knew to have used the services of prostitutes, among them an England international soccer player, and several clergymen.

The newspapers had another theory. They speculated that Tailford had fallen victim to a "homicidal maniac." Soon that premise would begin to gain traction.

On April 8, 1964, another naked body was fished from the Thames. She was Irene Lockwood, a 26-year-old prostitute, who'd last been seen alive in Chiswick the previous evening. She had been strangled with a ligature, probably fashioned from her own clothing.

The police soon discovered a number of reasons why someone might have wanted Irene Lockwood dead. A year earlier, Lockwood's close friend, Vicki Pender, had been found battered to death in her North London flat. Pender was found to have been involved in trying to blackmail her clients with photographs she'd taken of them, and Lockwood did not appear averse to similar scams. In fact, she was known to run a ruse where she'd ask her client to leave his clothes outside of the bedroom. Then, while she and the client had sex, an accomplice would emerge from hiding and go through the man's pockets, robbing him of cash and valuables.

As police continued their enquiries, another promising lead emerged. While searching Lockwood's apartment, they found a business card with the name "Kenny" on it, along with a telephone number. "Kenny" turned out to be Kenneth Archibald, a 57-year-old, former soldier and now caretaker at the Holland Park Tennis Club. Digging further the police discovered that Archibald ran an illegal late-night speakeasy from the caretaker's quarters at the club. Such illicit drinking clubs were common in London at the time, but Archibald offered his clientele more than just late night drinks. He also offered the services of ladies of the night, among them, Irene Lockwood.

Archibald was questioned by police and at first denied knowing Lockwood. However, after he was brought to Notting Hill police station for interrogation, he did an abrupt u-turn. Not only did he admit knowing Lockwood, he surprised officers by blurting, "I killed her. I have got to tell somebody about it."

He then went on to describe how he and Lockwood had gotten into an argument over money. "I must have lost my temper," he said, "I put my hands around her throat. I then proceeded to take her clothes off and rolled her into the river. I took her clothes home and burned them."

Archibald was arrested for the Lockwood murder, but senior investigators found it difficult to believe that this bumbling old man with the hearing aid, was the serial killer they sought. Within three days of Archibald's "confession" this belief was validated when a fifth naked body turned up in an alleyway in Brentford.

Helen Barthelemy, 22-years-old at the time of her death, had been strangled, and despite the location of the body, away from the river and a few miles from the others, police were in no doubt that it was part of the series. Like the other victims, Barthelemy was a streetwalker of slight stature who was suffering from an STD. She'd also acquired a police record for activities other than prostitution, having been arrested for luring a man to an isolated spot then robbing him with a straight razor. She had frequented many of the same pubs and speakeasies as Irene Lockwood and had possibly known her.

Other than the location in which Barthelemy's body was found there was one significant difference to the offers. The body was filthy, suggesting that it might have been stored somewhere before being dumped in the alley. There was also a promising clue, microscopic specks of different colored paint on her skin. Analysis of the paint revealed that it was the type used to spray cars and other metal work. From this, detectives concluded that the body might have been hidden in a building close to a spray-painting workshop since this kind of paint can be carried on the air and can penetrate gaps in walls and doors.

While the police focused their attention in narrowing down the possible locations of such workshops, extra officers were assigned to patrol along the Thames. Such patrols had, in fact, been stepped up after the Lockwood murder. But no sooner had that trap been set than Helene Barthelemy's body was found away from the river. It was almost as though the killer knew what the police would do next.

Meanwhile, Commander George Hatherill, head of Scotland Yard's CID had assumed overall control of the case. On April 28, 1964, he took the unusual step of making a public appeal to prostitutes to come forward with information. Given their inherent distrust of the police, it may have been expected the appeal would fall on deaf ears. However, such was the level of fear among streetwalkers that within a couple of days, 45 women had come forward.

Another initiative that Hatherill put in place was the documenting of all license plate numbers of cars seen in areas frequented by prostitutes. A number of decoys were also set up in these areas, female officers dressed as hookers in an effort to flush out the killer.

Prostitutes, for their part, were not relying solely on the police for protection. Many armed themselves with knives in the hope of fending off an attack. 30-year-old Scot, Mary Fleming, a veteran of over 10 years on the streets, certainly carried one, and boasted to her colleagues about how she'd once fought off a client who tried to strangle her.

When her naked body was found in Chiswick in the early hours of June 14, 1964, there were signs that she had indeed put up a fight. In the end, though, it had done her no good. She'd been strangled, stripped and dumped. As in the case of Helen Barthelemy, tiny particles of industrial paint were found on the body.

The location of the dump site, on a residential street in an area where the police presence was heaviest, seemed to highlight the killer's arrogance. The prevailing view amongst the investigators was that this was not coincidental, but a deliberate attempt to make the police look stupid. They began to wonder whether that might not be the underlying motive behind the crimes.

Meanwhile, the press had dubbed the elusive killer as "Jack The Stripper," an obvious pun on the name of the most notorious serial killer of all time. "The Stripper" had already equaled the body count of his deadly namesake. The pressure was mounting on detectives to catch him before he killed again.

In July 1964, Kenneth Archibald went on trial for the murder of Irene Lockwood. He had since retracted his confession, claiming that he had been drunk and depressed when he'd made it. With no other evidence against him, he was acquitted. The investigators close to the case had never considered him a viable suspect anyway.

The summer of 1964 passed without further incident, but London's prostitute population continued to be on alert. Most still went around armed with knives, while many had taken to working in pairs for extra security. They may have believed that such measures would keep them safe from the Stripper. On October 23, they were proved wrong in that assumption.

Frances Brown was a 21-year-old hooker from Edinburgh. On the night of October 23, she was drinking in a Notting Hill pub with her friend, Kim Taylor. The two had teamed up to watch over each other and as they prepared to hit the streets for the evening, they joked about their chances of running into the killer. Later, they were approached by two punters and split up to get into separate cars.

When Brown failed to return, Taylor contacted the police, telling them that her friend got into either a Ford Zephyr or Zodiac. A month would pass before Frances Brown's body was found on a Kensington side street on November 25th. The killing bore all the hallmarks of Jack The Stripper; Brown was small in stature and was found stripped and strangled, with telltale paint spots on the body.

But at least the police now had an eyewitness description of the killer. Kim Taylor described a round-faced man of medium height and solid build. Psychologists suggested that he was likely to be a meek individual who deliberately sought out petite women, as they were easier to overpower.

By none of this got police any closer to catching the killer. By the beginning of 1965 they had interviewed thousands of people and examined hundreds of leads, and still The Stripper was at large. It was only a matter of time before he struck again.

On February 16, 1965, the naked body of a 28-year-old Irish hooker named Bridie O'Hara was found behind a storage shed on an industrial estate in Acton. This was less than a mile from where Mary Fleming had been dumped.

The news had barely hit the headlines when Scotland Yard announced a new lead investigator on the case. Detective Chief Superintendent John Du Rose had a phenomenal resolution record. Nicknamed "Four Day Johnny" for the speed with which he usually solved cases, he immediately doubled the number of officers working the case.

Every vehicle traveling around West London during the hours of darkness had its details logged, and any car found "curb crawling" for prostitutes was put on a special watch list. In addition, Du Rose stepped up the hunt for the site where the bodies had been kept.

This search eventually paid off when a matching paint sample was found beneath a covered transformer on the Heron Trading Estate. It was just yards from where the body of Bridie O'Hara had been discovered. As the investigators had suspected, the premises faced a spray-painting workshop.

The killer's hideout had been found, but with over 7, 000 people employed on the trading estate, the police still had a lot of work to do. They began simultaneously conducting interviews and matching license plate numbers against those they had on their lists. Soon they'd whittled that list down to three suspects and Du Rose confidently predicted that they'd soon have their man.

For whatever reason, the arrest never came. Clearly, Du Rose's optimism had been misplaced and the killer had escaped the police dragnet. But the operation had not been entirely a failure. There were no further murders after the killing of Bridie O'Hara.

Still, the question remains. Who was Jack the Stripper?

Five years after the last murder, in 1970, John Du Rose gave an interview to BBC television. In it, the by-now retired detective claimed that he knew the identity of Jack The Stripper. He said that his detectives had been preparing to make an arrest when the suspect had committed suicide, gassing himself in a lock-up garage in South West London.

In his 1971 biography, Murder Was My Business, Du Rose repeated his claim, saying that the police strategy had been to use the media to scare the man into giving himself up. Instead, the killer had taken his own life, leaving a note, which said that he was "unable to take the strain any longer." Du Rose failed to name the suspect, referring to him only as "Big John."

Author Brian McConnell (in his 1974 book on the case, Found Naked And Dead) names the same suspect, saying he was a respectable man in his 40s, with a wife and several children. He was born in Scotland and had had a tough upbringing, marred by physical abuse. While serving in World War Two, he began using prostitutes and was known to turn violent when he'd been drinking. After the war, he became a police officer, but he quit after he was turned down for promotion to detective. He found work as a security guard, but harbored a deep resentment towards the police force over its perceived rejection of him. Part of the motive for the crimes was to humiliate the police. John had been a security guard at the Heron Trading Estate at the time of the murders. He had committed suicide shortly after the Bridie O' Hara murder.

On the face of it, "Big John" looks like a viable suspect, and for years, the version of events put forward by Du Rose and McConnell was accepted as true. But in 1972, author David Seabrook began researching the case, for a book that would later be released as Jack Of Jumps. Granted unprecedented access to the original case files, Seabrook spent several years on painstaking research. His conclusion was to roundly reject Du Rose's suspect.

According to Seabrook, the man suspected by Du Rose was Mungo Ireland, a Scot living in Putney at the time of the murders. Ireland could not have been the killer, he says, because he was in Scotland at the time of the Bridie O'Hara murder. Furthermore, there was very little evidence to link Ireland to the murders. He worked at the Heron Trading Estate for a period of only three weeks and there are no links to any of the other crimes. Most notably his license plate number was never recorded in the areas the police had under surveillance.

Ireland was found dead in his car on 3 March 1965. His suicide note read:

"I can't stick it any longer. It may be my fault but not all of it. I'm sorry Harry is a burden to you. Give my love to the kid.
Farewell,
Jock.
PS. To save you and the police looking for me I'll be in the garage."

Much has been made of that last line. Why would he assume that the police would be looking for him? It turns out he was due in court that morning on a minor traffic offense. The reference he makes to "my fault," likely refers to the marital problems his wife admitted they were having.

So if Seabrook rejects "Big John" as a suspect, who does he think was Jack the Stripper? Seabrook believes another former police officer to be the killer, a younger man than "Big John" who also had reason to hold a grudge against the police.

Seabrook's suspect was dismissed from the force in the early 1960s after being convicted of a series of burglaries in the area he patrolled. His motive for the murders was similar to the one Du Rose put forward for "Big John" - to humiliate the police by committing crimes that they would not be able to solve. Seabrook backs up his claim by pointing out that the last six bodies (Elizabeth Figg and Gwynneth Rees were never officially considered part of the series) were each found in different police sub-divisions. Very few people would be aware of these jurisdictions, other than a police officer. Seabrook's suspect had worked in all but one of them.

But even if Seabrook is correct, how does he explain why this suspect suddenly stopped killing? According to Seabrook, the old London police boundaries were changed in April 1965, thus removing his motive. This theory fails to convince. A serial killer, particularly one with at least six murders behind him, rarely stops killing of his own accord, and certainly not for such an arbitrary reason.

More than half a century since the first body turned up on the banks of the Thames, Jack the Stripper, like his infamous namesake, remains a phantom.

For more True Crime books by Robert Keller please visit

http://bit.ly/kellerbooks

Made in the USA
Las Vegas, NV
03 January 2023

64912033R00085